Chasing Snaps

Snapsvisor — Sweden's unique tradition

BY GÖRAN RYGERT

NORDSTJERNAN

FÖRLAG, NEW YORK

Chasing Snaps-Songs: The history, stirring incidents and adventures of the snapsvisan
©2013 Göran Rygert and Nordstjernan Förlag
ISBN: 0-9672176-9-7
First Edition
Printed in the United States of America

Nordstjernan Förlag
Book Services
P.O. Box 1710
New Canaan, CT 06840

NORDSTJERNAN Förlag, New York 2013
Cover and book design by Daniel Berubé-Arbello
Thank you for participating: Janet Rygert (pages 16, 18, 19, 20, 37); Patrik Björling Rygert (pages 16, 19, 37); Bertil Martinsson, Ove Engström, Torsten Arnbro (page 18); Ann-Catrin Forssberg, Niklas Björling Rygert (pages 37, 38).

Contents

7 ... Author's Note

11 ... History

13 ... What were they drinking?

15 ... Skål Rituals

16 ... Manners

17 ... Do's and Don'ts

23 ... The Masters

28 ... Helan Går

33 ... The Singing

33 ... Uniquely Swedish!

39 ... Stories from Swedish Universities & Colleges

47 ... Collections & Competitions

51 ... Create Your Own Snapsvisa

55 ... Drinking Rules & Motto

55 ... Snapsvisor and women

56 ... Snaps and sex

59 ... Snapsvisor in Swedish

73 ... Snapsvisor in English

79 ... Snapsvisor by Swedish Celebrities

85 ... Snapsvisor for Those Not Drinking

91 ... Synonyms of Snaps

95 ... Spicing the Snaps

98 ... Sources

101 ... Alphabetic list of songs

Author's Note

What is the similarity between bumblebees,
lonely cows and tinnitus?

Answer: You can find these as well as many other strange topics
in well-known Swedish snaps songs. (See "Bumblebees" page
73, "En droppe vatten" page 60, and "It's a Long Way" page 75)

And what's the difference between drinking more
than you should and being — almost — sober?

Answer: The snaps song!

If you ever plan to join a Swedish dinner party there's something you should know. Singer or not, there are occasions when everyone in Sweden makes his or her voice heard singing. Snaps, known also as schnapps, is a very important part of social gatherings in Sweden, as is the singing that usually accompanies the snaps. We will in this book adhere to the Swedish spelling snaps and to the extent possible *snapsvisa* for snaps song and *snapsvisor* for snaps songs. (*Nubbe*, page 92, and *nubbevisa* are just as common in the Swedish language.)

The singing of snaps songs and other songs at a party (which in Sweden often equals a dinner party) is fun and keeps you focused. The singing is equal to and fosters good manners. There is a Swedish song called "Dåne liksom åskan bröder" in which there is a line saying "Sången ädla känslor föder" (From singing comes noble feelings). That's exactly what happens when you sing snaps songs! The singing has a magic effect on Swedish dinner parties.

In a snaps song from Chalmers[1] is a line saying: "Så jag blir nog glad idag" (So I'll be glad today). To sing "Så jag blir nog full idag" (So I'll be drunk today) is a serious no-no.

When it comes to the toasting it is not necessary to drink a lot — or even have snaps in your glass. Many people do the toast with an alcohol-free beverage in their glass. But the singing is important. The unwritten rule is that you don't drink until you have

---

[1] ... Chalmers University of Technology, Göteborg, Sweden.

executed a snaps song first. This is especially important when the first snaps is poured into your glass. You do not even touch the glass until the first song has been sung!

The importance of the snaps song to sobriety is a matter open to discussion. But Sweden's most famous author, August Strindberg (1849-1912), made his opinion clear. Once in Paris in 1883 he invited some literary friends for dinner. On the invitation was made clear that four snaps songs had to be sung during the dinner. One of them was a travesty on Gunnar Wennerberg's "Oh, God Who Decides People's Fate."

The text of the snaps song ended with:

> *Den (snapsen alltså) är dess (folkets) skydd*
> *i gula faror,*
> *dess tröst i varje bleklagd sorg,*
> *den skyddar oss mot mask i magen*
> *och river som en tolvtumsspik.*

> *It (the snaps) is its (the people's) protection*
> *from yellow dangers,*
> *its consolation in each pale-faced sorrow,*
> *it protects us against worms in the stomach*
> *and it rasps as a twelve-inch nail.*

Another famous Swedish author and member of the Swedish Academy, Albert Engström (1869-1940), once wrote about an old dean who said: "In my home there is never any alcohol. But occasionally I have a geneva."

Parties where the snaps song prevails work like at the dean's house. There is no need for a lot of snapses, but maybe one or two preferably deliciously spiced shots.

The great Swedish-Finnnish author, Johan Ludvig Runeberg (1804-1877), once wrote about a man named Peter: "The sensible Peter did not — neither self, nor his esteemed brother-in-law — forget to take the morning snaps (*morgonsupen*), so they drank and stayed warm during their journey." Doctors at that time used to explain that one or two snapses at breakfast is most healthy because the alcohol sets the gastric juices in a good motion.

Finally, if someone declares: "I don't like snaps," you answer: "Right, who doesn't like a snaps!"

Göran Rygert, Atlanta in June 2013

History

Olaus Magnus: A history of the Nordic People

The Swedish custom of drinking snaps with a meal is deeply rooted in the souls of Swedes. This tradition goes back to the Middle Age. In the Old Norse saga it's told that even the god Thor spoke about the "bior" (beer) that was provided in Valhalla. And during the Viking Age people drank toasts to these gods of the Nordic mythology.

The Icelandic sagas described how they drank to Oden and other gods. They drank from the same bowl. During the Middle Ages craft guilds and order-like brotherhoods had rules describing how the bowl should be passed around, starting with the oldest man. It was very important that everyone had the same quantity to drink as they passed the vessel all around the table, or all around the company (*laget om*), or "lagom." It is from here the Swedish language got its expression "lagom," meaning not too much, not too little — just right!

These guilds had a religious touch and they cheered for the memory of the Savior, the Virgin Mary and the saints. It was called "to drink memory." To "drink memory" was eventually replaced by "drinking toast" and the common bowl was put away.

This drinking the toast around the table could take an awful lot of time. It is said that a guest had time to leave to sleep for a while and when he returned the toast was still going on.

A French diplomat visited Sweden in 1634 and wrote in his diary about a wedding he attended. Everyone had to stand up and drink toasts for the king of France and the queen. Then they had to deliver a long speech for a table neighbor before the toast passed on. That took one and a half hours. Then people started to quarrel about whether everything should be repeated for the king of Spain. The party ended in the throwing of cups and glasses and it all went to pieces.

Violent drinking parties were common. When people were finished drinking they threw the stoup away. The stoups were mainly made of tin. But soon people started drinking from glasses. When King Erik XIV in 1563 hosted a Christmas party for Stockholm's bourgeois, 174 crystal glasses were crushed. It was not any better for his brother, King Johan III, who in 1573 got 375 glasses broken.

Even if the toasting had a religious background, the bishops, after the Reformation, complained about the unchristian drinking habits in the guilds. So, how much did they drink? In the 16th century, three to four liters of beer (about one gallon) was considered absolutely necessary every day. Rich people probably consumed even more because they also drank wine.

Feelings have often run high in Sweden when the people's right to its snaps was questioned. (Left) "Crayfish require these drinks – Vote no"; The famous poster by Albert Engström prior to a referendum on the prohibition of alcohol on August 27, 1922. (Voter turnout was 55.1%, and the suggestion failed by 51% against 49%.)

What were they drinking?

Beer is the oldest drink we know, next to water. It has been brewed for thousands of years. Beer was the ceremonial drink when people settled affairs such as marriage or inheritance. Without the beer a document was not legal and the agreement not binding. The beer was the center at all kinds of events. In the Swedish language, in which the word for beer is "öl," there are also still words such as "gravöl" (funeral feast) and "taklagsöl" (topping-out party, on completion of the framework for the roof of a new building).

Wine was a luxury. Only members of the royal court and rich burghers could afford it.

Water was something people were suspicious of — it's no wonder, considering the lack of hygiene of those times. The water was not always particularly clean. In a book printed in the 18th century a Swedish farmer wrote: "Water is drunk by all dumb animals that rarely get anything else to drink."

Coffee and tea (and chocolate) did not show up in Sweden until the end of the 18th century.

Alcohol could — in the 15th century — be used only for the manufacturing of gunpowder. But one hundred years later it became a luxury beverage. At first it could only be bought at pharmacies, as medicine to drink in small dosages for the improvement of health. It was considered good for plague, gout, boils, headache, gallstones, stomachache and much more. And snaps spiced with wormwood is still considered good for your stomach.

In the 18th century snaps became more and more common — to such a degree that a ban against making moonshine was issued in 1718. However, this ban did not hold the dean Reinerus Broocman back; in a book from 1736 describing how the grain and the home distillery should be handled by the housekeeper, he says, "Next to God's blessing she should, from one barrel[I] of rye be able to get 18 to 20 tankards of good and strong Swedish snaps, after it has been mixed with fresh, good running water to its appropriate strength."

At the same time the drunkenness increased. In that connection the priests were not excluded. The rural vicarages served

---

[I]... One barrel (*tunna*) = 165 liter = 44 gallons. One tankard (*kanna*) = 2.6 liter = 0.7 gallon

both as farms and inns. There are many stories about priests who had too much of the good stuff. One of them was reported for "competing with drinking-brothers in the art of cursing and singing snaps songs." In the cities more and more places opened for people to stop for a drink. The number of restaurants, inns and taverns in Stockholm in 1754 was 723, equal to one for every 79 residents.

'Svenska folket' (The Swedish People) Drawing by Albert Engström.

And snaps became even more popular. In 1829, 22 million tankards were produced. That was five and a half gallons per inhabitant. There were hardly any exports of alcohol, so most of the snaps was consumed in Sweden, moonshine not included.

At threshing-time everyone in the country was treated to a so-called "morning-bite" at 3 a.m. It consisted of a piece of bread and snaps. And a snaps at this time was a glass holding at least 10 cl (3.3 ounces). The farmer himself then treated himself with a snaps — or two — with every meal.

Skål Rituals

'Ett Jungfrutal' Drawing by Albert Engström.

The ancient "drinking memory" was eventually replaced by "drinking a toast." The old wooden stoups were replaced by wooden bowls. The expression "att dricka en skål" (to drink a toast) probably came from "ênes schâle drinken," from the Low German language, which means to drink to someone's prosperity.

Besides all the toasting for the king they also toasted for everything they could come up with: parents, siblings, namedays, etc. It was extremely important to a person to accept a toast that was dedicated to him. Refusing could have ill-fated consequences.

A story from the 17th century tells about a man named Petter Nublikin who — at Baggens källare, a restaurant in Stockholm's Old Town — got killed with a knife after he refused to accept a toast from his "friend" Hans Trost Skinnare.

All toasts had to be drunk bottoms up. Carl von Linné, in his book from 1734, "Dalaresa," describes how the guests who visited a farm for the first time had to drink a toast from a special bowl, the so-called "welcome toast." It often held a lot and had to be emptied by the guest. Linné felt like "his stomach was about to burst, the head crack, and the health and all life's pleasure say good-bye!"

Manners

A Swedish book about manners, printed in 1936, tells us "Toasting is a must — thoroughly and orderly." Today orderly toasting is not always needed, but it is for sure still a must at fancier dinner parties with many participants. A foreigner described the Swedish toasting technique in a book in these words: "With your best Sunday look you lift your glass up to the level of an imaginary third uniform button, while staring the guest of honor in the white of his eyes. After doing this you are allowed to drink but you still have to look straight into his eyes. Then you can put down the glass. Everything must be with a facial expression of ceremoniously pleasant gravity, that for most foreigners would take years to learn."

You lift your glasses and look straight into your faces. Do not clink.

Put your glasses down. Do not look at each other anymore.

If you are a guest at a fancy dinner party you need to know what you can do and what you cannot do.

Do's and don'ts

❶ Do not touch your glass before the host takes hold of his, proposing a toast, greeting everyone to the table.

❷ After the welcoming toast, men are expected to begin toasting their lady to the right.

❸ A toast is usually between two people, unless specifically designated as general — welcoming spring, to the bridal couple, to the birthday child etc.

❹ No one is allowed to toast with the host.

❺ You are not to toast with the hostess of the evening if you are more than eight at the table.

❻ You never clink with your glasses — you do not even bring the glasses together.

❼ A man cannot toast with a man who is older or has a (much) higher rank or status.

❽ A lady never toasts with her cavalier.

These days it is not uncommon to overlook some of these rules, however. Most modern Swedish women will not hold back toasting a man, for instance.

In older days — certainly in the 1930s — it was good manners to empty your glass (a reminiscence from 300 to 400 years ago). Another observation from the 1930s is that you should not be drinking all evening along without any toasting. Today you may drink by yourself without proposing a toast, except that you should toast at least once with your lady on your right, your dinner partner.

In older days, during the dinner the host should have had to toast with all the ladies first and then with all the men, one by one, in both cases starting with the most distinguished. Today the hosts normally solve the problem by proposing a joint toast, an "allgemeines" or "allmän" (general) toast.

'Allmän' skål, a general toast where everyone participates.

When it comes to the snaps, ladies who do not drink are recommended to behave as if nothing was the matter and they should just continue eating, as recommended in the 1930s.

When you toast with the lady on your right you should lift your glass with your left hand in order to not be building a wall between the two of you with your right arm.

If a toast is proposed for everyone, the gentlemen turn first toward their dinner partners to their right and toast with her, then turn left and toast with the lady there. This is an old tradition that is still very much alive, certainly at fashionable dinner parties. At the pub or at informal dinners it is not that important what you do. You may even clink glasses.

If it happens that you would be invited for the great Nobel dinner at Stockholm's City Hall it would be good to know how to toast with the king. No, you don't move up behind him with a glass in your hand, tapping him on his shoulder saying: "Hey, your Majesty may I toast with you?" It won't work. Or maybe it will, but the security would quickly be there, showing you to the door.

When an official proposes a toast for the king, he says: "A toast to His Majesty, the King." Then everyone stands up and answers: "The King!" Thereafter they lift their glasses and drink. The toast must be in wine.

When it comes to beer, the rule is that you should not toast at all. But these days nobody really pays much attention to this rule.

Do not build a wall between yourself and your dinner partner...

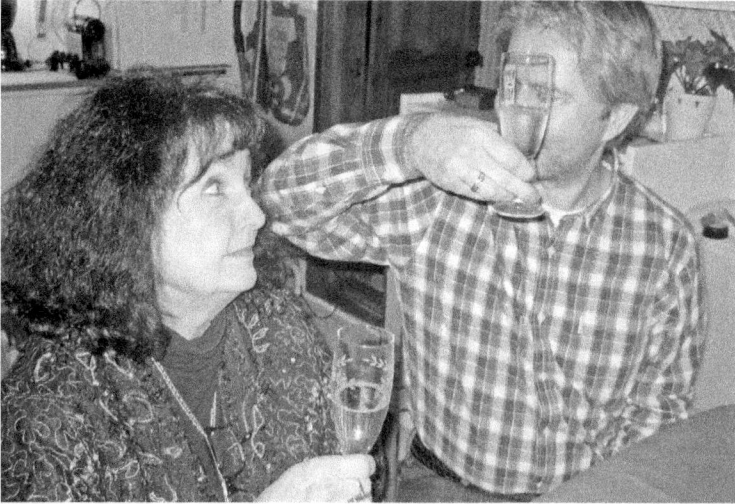

...she may get annoyed!

Good beer deserves a toast! At the very least, beer drinkers who just got their beer may mutter: "Well, here we go." Or, in Swedish just "Ja hej då," while lifting the glasses.

...if they drink from glasses! In the United States, people don't drink beer from glasses anymore — they drink from the bottle, even at grand dinners. Restaurants generally don't provide a glass unless you ask for one. And if you do, you might get a frosted glass that is so cold that you don't taste anything. All taste is effectively killed.

The beer culture in Sweden is somewhat better. The beer connoisseurs drink from glasses because they want to see the color

Beer tastes better from a nice glass.

of the beer and the foam in the glass. Not only that — beer, like wine, has aromas that get lost and will escape unnoticed when you drink from the bottle. A beer tastes so much better from a beautiful, thin glass, such as a one from Stella Artois! And it must not be served colder than 50 to 59 F° (10 to 15 C°) — a lighter beer somewhat colder than a darker. If the beer is colder than that the flavor gets destroyed. However, if you don't care how your beer tastes I can't help you!

Likewise, good, spiced snaps must not be served colder than 53 to 59 F° (12 to 15 C°). The tradition of cooling the snaps in the freezer comes from the fact that cheap, unseasoned snaps often has a raw taste that won't be felt if it's ice cold. So, please do not destroy the taste of your nicely spiced snaps.

When it comes to the toasting it is not necessary to drink a lot, or even have snaps in your glass. Many people do the toast with an alcohol-free beverage. But the singing is important. The unwritten rule is you don't drink until you have first sung a snaps song. This is especially important when the first snaps is poured. You do not even touch the glass before the first snaps song is executed!

The importance of the snaps song to sobriety is a matter open to discussion. But Sweden's most famous author, August Strindberg (1849-1912), had a clear opinion: In Paris in 1883, he invited some cultural friends for dinner, making certain in the invitation that four snaps songs had to be sung during dinner. One of them was a travesty on Swedish Academy member Gunnar Wennerberg's "Oh, God Who Decides People's Fate." You find the lyrics under Author's notes on page 9.

Another famous Swedish author, and member of the Swedish Academy, Albert Engström (1869-1940), once wrote about an old dean who said, "In my home there is never any alcohol. But occasionally I have a genever (Belgian gin)."

Parties where the snaps songs prevail are like those at the dean's house — there is no need for a lot of snaps, but maybe one or two preferably deliciously spiced shots.

Swedish-Finland's great author, Johan Ludvig Runeberg (1804-1877), once wrote about a man called Peter: "The sensible Peter did not — neither self, nor his esteemed brother-in-law — forget to take the morning snaps (morgonsupen), so they drank and stayed warm during their journey." Doctors at that time used to explain that one or two snaps at breakfast was most healthy because the alcohol sets the gastric juices in a good motion. Finally, if someone declares, "I don't like snaps," remember to answer, "Right, who doesn't like a snaps!"

The Masters

Bellman

In the 18th century we had Carl Michael Bellman (1740-1795). He was a poet and composer, much appreciated by King Gustaf III who called him "Mr. Improviser." Bellman is a central figure in the Swedish song tradition and remains a very important influence in Swedish music, as well as in Scandinavian literature in general. Bellman was also a good singer and accompanied himself on a cister, a flat-bottomed stringed instrument. Many of his songs were drinking songs and several of them are still included in Sweden's vast repertoire of drinking songs, such as "Vila vid denna källa" and "Bort allt vad oro gör."

With "Gustafs skål," an informal royal anthem, Bellman acquired Gustav III's patronage (from "Dikter till Gustaf III och Konungahuset"). The melody was very well known during the end of the 18th century, but it was not Bellman's own composition.

Gustafs skål

UR DIKTER TILL GUSTAF III OCH KONUNGSHUSET

*Revolutionskvällen den 19 augusti 1772, när Gustaf III lyckligt
genomfört sin oblodiga statsvälvning, hyllade Bellman på
Skeppsholmen den segrande monarken med denna sång.*

Marche — Carl Michael Bellman

Gus - tafs skål! Den bäs - te kung, som nor - den ä - ger:
Han ej tål, att vikt - skåln o - jämt vä - ger.
God och glad, han il - skans röst för - ak - tar
samt av - vak - tar och be - trak - tar dår - skap i sin grad.

Sådan kung
är värd att styra Sveriges öden:
rask och ung,
ej rådlös uti nöden.
Vasa ätt
har aldrig lärt att svika,
aldrig tvika
men att fika
till att göra rätt.

Brännvinslåten

Sång för halfvan från Mora, att lika glädtigt som allvarligt sjungas, upptäckt af Zorn, upptecknad af Carl Göran Nyblom.

Få, få, få, få, fåmi li te upp i ko su, få, få, få, få, fåmi li te upp i ko su'

Jen gång å jen gång å jen gång å jen gång tel Tra-lal-la lal-lal-la tral-lal-la lal-la-la'

Följande vers tillägnas FÖRENINGEN MORA BYGDELAG av E. Arkö att i samma sinnelag sjungas till halvan.

> Wånt'n smörå,
> Supen litter upp umörå,
> Jän fåmi jenn til,
> Känn[x], an värm i kvidim, 'ken[x] will
> Undvår jen sup til å nejk för jenn lisslan til?
> Tralala, lalala, tralala, lalala.

[x] i båda fallen hårt k.

Översättning

Få, få, få, få
Låt oss få litet i kåsan! :/
En gång och en gång och en gång och en gång till
Tralala, lalala, tralala, lalala.

Osten, smöret,
Supen lättar upp humöret.
Här få vi en till.
Känn, han värmer i magen. Vem vill
undvara en sup till och neka att ta en till?
Tralala, lalala, tralala, lalala.

The history of Sweden and its cultural elite is filled with references to the singing. This nubbevisa was originally discovered by world renowned artist Anders Zorn in the early 20th century. Shared courtesy of Kerstin Alm whose family from the Dalarna province kept a copy intact through the years.

Gustafs Skål

Gustafs skål! Den bäste kung som norden äger.
Han ej tål att viktskåln ojämt väger.
God och glad, han ilskans röst föraktar
samt avvaktar och betraktar dårskap i sin grad.

A toast for Gustaf! The best king in the north.
He can't stand that the scales are uneven.
Nice and happy, he despises the voice of anger
and watches and looking for folly.

Here are two examples of Bellman's drinking songs:

Hej! fram med öl och tallestrunt
(From "Bacchanaliska visor")

Hej! fram med öl och tallestrunt,[1]
det är ju magesunt.
Trumla och tumla och drick utur rågade mått;
hoppa och troppa till Bacchi[2] slott.

Lät oss då supa laget om runt,
blodet är rent och tunt.
Trumla och mumla, ännu är couraget[3] gott;
hoppa och troppa till Bacchi slott.

Hey! Come out with beer and snaps (pine-sprout rubbish),
that is good for your stomach.
Barrel and tumble and drink from heaped bowls;
hop and go in troops to Bacchus' palace.

Let us drink, let's go the round,
The blood is clean and thin.
Tumble and mumble, the spirits are still good;
hop and go in troops to Bacchus' palace.

1... *Tallestrunt* was the name of the snaps that was spiced with the light green sprout from the pine-tree (*tall* = pine).
2... Bacchus is the Roman name for Dionysus, the god of wine.
3... The mood.

Har du något i flaskan kvar

(Fredman's Song #59)

Har du något i flaskan kvar?
Hurra, så lät oss då lustiga supa!
Har du något i flaskan kvar, kära far!
Häll då i glaset för envar, kära far,
häll kära far,
lät det då rinna medan du har.
Håll, kära far, håll, kära far,
nog av denna spiritus för vår torstiga strupa.
Klinga, gubbar, glas mot glas,
lät oss då leva medan vi kunna,
lät oss friskt om kransen⁣ dras,
rida med Bacchus på tunna.
Sitter du trumpen vankas det stryk;
Aj, aj, aj aj, aj, aj, aj, aj.
Sitter du blyger, ränn då och ryk!
Aj, aj, aj, aj, aj, aj, aj, aj
Drick i botten som en karl,
världen han vill oss det unna.

⟆... Kransen = the victory wreath, Bacchus' reward, that is the booze, intoxication.

Do you have anything left in the bottle?
Hurray, then let us drink and have fun!
Do you have anything left in the bottle, dear father!
Then fill up the glass for everyone, dear father,
pour, dear father,
let it flow while you have.
Enough, dear father, enough, dear father,
enough of this spirit for our thirsty throats.
Clink, fellows, glass to glass,
let us live while we can,
let us fast get the wreath,
ride with Bacchus on the barrel.
If you sit there sulky you are in for a thrashing;
Ay, ay ,ay ,ay ,ay ,ay, ay, ay.
If you sit there shy, run around!
Ay, ay, ay, ay, ay, ay, ay, ay.
Drink bottoms up as a man,
the world will not begrudge us.

The Bellman joke is a type of simple joke always including a person named Bellman as the main character. The first known Bellman jokes survive in a book from 1835, which quotes a Bellman joke in a letter written 1808 by a contemporary of Bellman. 19th century Bellman jokes tended to focus on C.M. Bellman's life at the court. Since then, however, the Bellman character of the jokes has changed into a generic person, rather than the historical figure. The shift from jokes told by adults to jokes told mainly by school children up to 10 years of age probably happened in the first half of the 20th century. The modern versions of the Bellman jokes often include Bellman and two other characters of different nationalities, with the former coming out victorious from a tricky situation.

Here is one of them: A Dane, a Norwegian and Bellman made a wager on who could remain inside a goat pen the longest. First out was the Dane, who came out after just 10 minutes yelling, "Damn! The goat stinks!" After him the Norwegian went in, and after half an hour he came out yelling, "Damn! The goat stinks!" Finally Bellman went in. After two hours the goat came rushing out yelling, "Damn! Bellman stinks!"

Helan   *Halvan*

Helan Går

Helan går, sjung hopp, faderallan lallan lej.
Helan går, sjung hopp, faderallan lej.
Och den som inte helan tar
han heller inte halvan får.
Helan går!
Sjung hopp, faderallan lej!

This almost 200-year-old Swedish drinking song has, to non-Swedes, become more well-known than the Swedish National Anthem. The origin of this melody may have been from older trumpet signals. The first evidence is from 1843 when the Swedish composer Frans Berwald (1796-1868) used the first four bars of "Helan går" when writing his operetta "Modehandlerskan." The operetta was first performed at the Royal Opera in Stockholm on March 26, 1845, but it became a fiasco. "Helan går" was at the time already well-known. That it indeed was quoted in the operetta is proved from the orchestra musicians who are said to have expressed their clear disapproval, when hearing those four bars. They thought they were indecorous.

"Helan går" became more and more used. From the end of the 19th century, stories are told about how the soldiers sang "Helan går" while having a breakfast, consisting of sandwiches with beer and snaps. Sweden's great author August Strindberg (1849-1912) compared "Helan går" with Sweden's national anthem, in his diary in which he tells about how people at a breakfast buffet "stand up and sing 'the national anthem' Helan går."

HELAN GÅR
"HELAN"
Musik & text: Helan går

He - lan går, sjung hopp, fa - de - ral - lan - lal - lan lej! He - lan går, sjung hopp, fa - de - ral - lan lej! Och den som in - te He - lan tar, han in - te hel - ler Hal - van får. He - lan går! Sjung hopp, fa - de - ral - lan lej!

Frans Lehár (1870-1948) visited Sweden in 1936 when his opera Greven av Luxemburg (The Count of Luxembourg) was performed in Stockholm. While attending a crawfish party he heard a song he liked a lot, during which people were standing at strict attention, singing solemnly.

Back home in Vienna he went to the Swedish embassy, trying to find out what song it was. There he was told that it was not the Swedish national anthem he had heard — it was "Helan går." Shortly thereafter Lehár wrote five variations of the song, all in different states of minds.

He called them:

❶ "In vornehmer Gesellschaft" ("In Dignified Company")

❷ "Bei schlechter verärgeter Laune" ("In a Bad, Irritated Mood")

❸ "In verliebler Stimmung" ("In the Mood For Love")

❹ "In etwas alkoholisierter Stimmung (Nur für Männer)" ("Somewhat Under the Influence (For men only)")

❺ "In fröhlicher übermütiger Stimmung" ("In High Spirits")

The five variations are now arranged for men's choir and are available from Vasa Drängar, Atlanta.

Here is an example of how people use "Helan går." During my time at Chalmers University of Technology in Göteborg I was involved in "spex", a sort of funny, burlesque student theater. At one of our performances in the town of Erlangen in southern Germany we had many Danish people in the audience. After the final encores and applause, the Danes stood up and sang "Helan går" in unison — to our homage. It was their way of showing their appreciation.

Another example: In 1957 the Swedish hockey team "Tre Kronor" won the World Championship Gold Medal in Moscow. The Russians had not prepared any recording of the Swedish National Anthem "Du gamla du fria" because they were very sure of winning the championship. So the Swedish heroes and champions were asked to sing it without any accompaniment. They however did not remember the words so instead they sang "Helan går."

There are many versions of this popular song, in other languages, as follows:

Transliteration
Hal and Gore,
shun hop, father Alan Lalan ley.
Hal and Gore, shun hop, father Alan ley.
Oh handsome in the hell and tar
an' Hal are in the half and four.
Hal and Gore,
shun hop, father Alan ley.

Translation to English
Now for the first.
Sing hop, faderallan lallan ley.
Now for the first. Sing hop, faderallan ley.
And those who won't the first one take
they also number two forsake.
Now for the first.
Sing hop, faderallan lallan ley.

Pig Latin
E lancor,
sien gopfa de rala ralala,
e lancor, siun gopfa de ralala.
Odense nunte e lancar
aninte eler alvan for.
E lancor!
Sium gopfa de rala la!

Russian

Vodka zdyes,
poy poy, tra-la-la-la la-la la.
Vodka zdyes, poy poy, tra-la-la-la la.
Kto pervoy rumotchki nye pyot,
vtoroy naprasna zdyot da zdyot.
Vodka zdyes!
Poy poy, tra-la-la-la la!

Japanese

Tomodachi,
ippai, ippai, nomimasho.
Tomodachi, ippai, nomimasho.
Moshi ippai o nominasen
nihai o moraimasen.
Tomodachi!
Ippai, ippai, nomimasho!

The Singing

Community singing as it relates to the drinking of alcoholic beverages is fairly ageless. Early Greeks and Romans sang to the toast. The Swedes have been singing songs to the toast for 500 years. Many of the songs came from continental Europe and England. Above all, most influences came from Germany. Many visiting or immigrant Germans brought manners and customs, such as maypoles, Walpurgis Night bonfires and more.

However, in none of the imported songs, not even in Bellman's production (see page 23) is the word "snaps" mentioned. That word is to be found for the first time in 1799, many years after Bellman's death. The true snaps song debuted in the 19th century. In their songs, Bellman and other poets wrote about the drinking of beer, wine and alcoholic beverages; but those songs are not what we today call "snapsvisor."

Before 1850, the Swedish songs to the toasts were actually not very Swedish. Their origin was mostly from German and French traditions. Some of them were plain translations.

During the 19th century, though, snaps became Sweden's favorite beverage, and the Swedish snaps song was born at the Swedish snaps table. Shots of the "appetite snaps" were taken when eating from the typical Swedish smörgåsbord. At this time women were not allowed to drink snaps, therefore we can assume the authors of the early snaps songs were all male.

Uniquely Swedish

"The Snaps Song is not only typical Swedish, it is uniquely Swedish."

This is a statement by folklorist and song researcher Christina Mattson[I], who in 2002 published, "Från Helan till lilla Manasse, the history of the Swedish snaps song." Drinking songs can be found all over the world, but snaps songs are only in Sweden and in the parts of Finland where Swedish is spoken. A few have indeed been found in Denmark and Norway, but they all have shown to be translated from Swedish. Snaps-singing never got a foothold in these countries' traditions, but Swedes became more and more interested in snapsvisor. Already in the first half of the 19th century they were numbered Helan (the First), Halvan (the Second) and Tersen (the

---

[I]... One of the main sources for this book.

'Quartet' Drawing by C.A. Dahlström

Third). And the expansion of this systematics continued. Today no less than 20 snapses are numbered and named (page 58).

Not only is "Helan går" (page 28) dated to the first half of the 19th century, but so is "Hej tomtegubbar" (page 62) — a must with the Christmas snaps — which is early in origin, printed in 1833. Early breeding grounds for the snaps song were the universities in Lund and Uppsala. The students loved to sing, during their studies as well as at parties of their "Nations" or Nationer[ɪ] in Swedish Choir singing in four parts became popular.

The famous men's choir Orphei Drängar was founded in Uppsala in 1833. Not only were songs to the snaps executed., but soon the students also began singing to the punsch, a low alcohol beverage that became incredibly popular at the universities during the 19th century. ("Punsch" is a traditional, very sweet

---

[ɪ]... A word about the Swedish phenomenon of the Student "Nation" — Nations are at the center of Lund or Uppsala social life. Think of them as a cross between fraternities, and the Harry Potter house system. Instead of 4 houses, in Lund there's 13, and you get to be the sorting hat yourself. Each of them is named after some region of Sweden (Lund, Malmö, Göteborg, etc.) Each has their own building, usually with some housing in it (for some, but definitely not all members of the nation) and an area or two to hold events, mostly pubs and clubs.

Swedish liqueur produced from arrack, neutral spirits, sugar, water and various flavorings. Arrack, originally a strong Indian liquor, was imported from Java and became the base ingredient for punsch.)

It has become a tradition for ensembles to drink to punsch while dressing and doing make-up. It is said to be good for improving the voice by clearing the throat; it also dampens nerves. But at Chalmers in the 1950s this imbibing of punsch was criticized by students who were not involved in the ensembles, called spex.

That gave rise to an interview with a representative of the spex ensemble. He said, "I strongly doubt that any of us in the spex ensemble would undergo rehearsals (at which at most a beer will be consumed) every evening during several weeks —possibly causing disfavor with wives and girlfriends — as well as other hardships — just for the pleasure of getting some free punsch during the week of performances. I don't know anyone with that disposition, however there are envious people. This punsch, that we call "behind the scenes punsch" has never caused any dampening of the atmosphere at the theater and the costs for it are always accrued by the ensemble members themselves."

Many songs are written to the punsch. One of the most popular songs is "Punschen kommer" (The Punsch Is Coming", see page 69).

The breakthrough of the snaps-singing happened among students when alcohol restrictions demanded food be served in connection with the drinking. That meant sit-down dinners.

No longer was it allowed to have a snaps while standing around a table. At about the same time, in the beginning of the 20th century, the singing in unison became popular and met the demand for longed-for solidarity.

Books with drinking songs were printed in the beginning of the 19th century. [Zorn] These books contained mostly literary songs, written by well-known Swedish authors who sometimes published them anonymously. In the 20th century, snaps songs collected from folk traditions were getting printed. The first came in 1910 at the University of Uppsala. Also at the university in Helsinki, the same year, a snaps songbook was printed, called "Vasungavisor."

Since then countless numbers of snaps songbooks have been issued, with or without music. In the 1990s alone about 20 were published.

Sometimes instructions on how to sing were included in them. Or how to handle the book: "At the singing the book should be held in the left hand and the glass with the right. For left-handed persons do the opposite or just anyhow."

Various snaps songbooks

Song sheets started to show up at small and large parties. They included older, well-known snaps songs and, sometimes new ones especially written for the occasion. They could be (the tradition continues today) songs for birthdays, parties for employees, weddings, holiday dinners, midsummer celebrations, crawfish parties, eel feasts, surströmming parties (parties where fermented Baltic herring is devoured), goose dinners (mostly in the province of Skåne!), housing associations, family celebrations, songs for a boat club, golf club or bus tour, and the list goes on. Songbooks and song sheets may also include different themes or subjects, such as in the following, drawn from a snaps song website:

Beer songs
Children's song melodies
Dirty songs

Herring songs
International songs
Punsch songs
Short songs
Songs for men and women
Songs for seniors
Songs for the day after
Songs to begin the party
Songs to end the party
Wine songs

To sing around the dinner table is a tradition deeply rooted in the hearts of the Swedish people. It is a part of the Swedish cultural heritage and the singing of snaps songs helps carry on the tradition. Those best at maintaining the tradition of singing snaps songs are the moderate drinkers.

What's important is atmosphere. If people are not in the mood for singing, there will be no spontaneous singing, even if there are songbooks or sheets on the table. Someone needs to initiate and lead the singing and then keep it going.

A purpose of the singing is entertainment — compared with the Irish tradition of writing limericks. Sometimes you wonder if the snaps is just an excuse for the pleasure of singing. When you have a snaps in front of you, just sip it to make sure it will last through three or four songs.

The singing of snapsvisor is not only extremely popular in Sweden, it is also important because the singing increases the atmosphere of the party and has a nice side effect, a matter of

Singing is fun, at smaller or greater parties.

At a party when you sing, no one runs the risk of ending up under the table!

temperance policy: You drink less because you are busy singing! Someone in a pleasant company drinks less than the one who sits in his boring loneliness. Also, the singing burns calories!

It was not long before the first snaps song was recorded. The year was 1906 and tenor Carl Gentzel recorded a snapsvisa called "Helan, halfran och tersen." (Note the old spelling of the word "halfran" which means "the second.")

Since then many Swedish singers and choirs, well-known or not, have made recordings of all kind of snaps- and drinking songs, on old 78 records, EPs, LPs and CDs. The only — so far — American CD recording of Swedish snaps songs is "Ta dej en jamare," recorded and issued in 2010 by the singing group "Qvartetten," Atlanta, GA.

Stories from Swedish and Finnish Universities

In the following you will see the words "Spex" and "Chalmers." Chalmers refers to Chalmers University of Technology in Göteborg, Sweden. Spex or student spex is a genuine Swedish tradition created in the 1860s and maintained at Swedish universities and colleges. It is a special kind of a stage production, a mix of theater, musical and historical farce, in which the subject is often an historic figure such as a king or famous person. The history is always re-interpreted and includes numerous anachronisms to make the story more fun. All female roles are performed by male actors. At the University of Lund there's one other student performance where female performers are included, called a pjäx – a hybrid of pjäs, meaning play, and a spex. Also, in an effort to achieve gender equality between Emil (the male students) and Emilia (the female students) at Chalmers a spex is produced every year with only female actors.

In 1952 Chalmers' spex ensemble had a new assistant stage manager. His duties were to provide simpler properties as well as beer and booze. During the liquor-ration book era new Chalmerists were often pretty unacquainted with alcohol, its manners and customs.

The only contact this assistant (whose name was not released) previously had with alcohol was restricted to seeing his father taking snaps at every Sunday dinner. The father consumed "Skåne," a snaps spiced with fennel, caraway and aniseed. The assistant thus took the collected liquor-ration book library, went to the "Systembolaget" (the Swedish monopoly booze seller) and bought 80 liters of Skåne, about 21 gallons. Nothing else. Only Skåne.

The ensemble was treated to make-up Skåne, after-performance Skåne, party Skåne and small-hours Skåne. At the end of the spex-performing week the assistant stood at the entrance of the make-up rooms serving a mandatory entry-Skåne. At the moment of parting in the evenings one could hear the line: "Would you like some Skåne to take home?" Not one of the members of the Chalmers spex ensemble has thereafter been seen drinking Skåne — unless there was no other option.

Many great songs have been written after an author was inspired by a small snaps. Or two. One example is the writing of the text for "Hustruvisan," included in the spex "Henry the Eight," at Chalmers in 1954. The three authors were in the vicinity of Göteborg, having rented a house as a place to spend the summer. These three guys were frequent blood donors and earned 28 Swedish crowns (about $5) per draw. With this earned money, a total of 84 Swedish crowns (about $15), they went to Systembolaget and bought a number of small (37 cl, about one tenth of a gallon) bottles ("but not too much of Skåne!") which were placed in public view on a window ledge — it was there for consumption and for getting needed inspiration, not only for "Hustruvisan" but for the entire "Henry the Eight" spex. The song "Hustruvisan" became so popular for many years that you would think it was a snapsvisa.

One of the famous snaps songs from Chalmers is "Ratataa," written in 1956 by a few Chalmerists who had seen Povel Ramel's new movie "Ratataa — or The Staffan Stolle Story." They gathered one morning at Chalmers' spex ensemble's club (it happened to be in the morning of the Lucia celebration) to write a text to the melody of "Ratataa." Inspiration, as well as a glass of black currant spiced snaps, turned up. At 11 a.m. the snaps song was ready to be sung for the very first time. Just as everyone stood with their glasses around the piano singing "Ratataa, now let's have a dram," the door opened and Chalmers' dean, together with Göteborg's bishop, peeped in. That became a visit which remains unequalled.

Numerous examples can be found on how authors of snapsvisor or casual texts got their inspiration. A technological student at Chalmers went through agonies over the subject of concrete technique. The professor was powerful and feared. The student was going to spend a night with a beautiful girl, but he could not give up the thought of concrete technique, and the date became a failure. Instead this unsuccessful affair became a song that won first prize in a literary competition.

Snapsvisor can be written everywhere. One became a classic after being written on a train — the author was on his way from Stockholm to a costume party in Göteborg. The party's theme was "Lanthushållningssällskapsfest år 1900" (Agriculture Association Festivity in 1900). The author managed to include the whole word "Lanthushållningssällskapsfester" in his song.

A radical step in the writing of snapsvisor was taken in the 1940s at KTH (The Royal Institute of Technology, Stockholm). In a song "Septen" (The Seventh) written by Pekka Norén, all spaces between words were eliminated so the text was reduced to one long word: "Nuskaviklämmaseptengutårklämmaentrudeluttom-detgårtjosanmuhammedsnartärdetvårjulaftonärenfreda."

LIVET ÄR HÄRLIGT
LIVET
UR CHALMERSSPEXET KATARINA II, 1959
CHALMERS SNAPSVISA TILL "HELAN" FRÅN 1960-TALET OCH FRAMÅT
Musik: Poljoschko-pole (Lev Knipper); Text: Bengt Åke "Bengå" Möller, V 52

Con spirito
Piano-intro. — Hela tiden crescendo *pp - ff*

Li - vet är här - ligt, ta - va - ritj, vårt liv är här - ligt, vi al - la vå - ra små be - kym - mer glöm - mer när vi har fått en tår på tand, en skål! Ta dej en vod - ka, ta - va - ritj, en li - ten vod - ka, gla - sen i bot - ten vi till - sam - mans töm - mer, det kom - mer me - ra ef - ter hand. hand. *Hej!*

One of Sweden's most famous and popular snapsvisor is "Livet är härligt" (Life Is A Pleasure/Leben ist herrlich).

It is the Crème de la Crème of snaps songs. It was written for Chalmers' spex Katarina II (Catherine the Second) in 1959. The audience loved it, so it had to be sung as an encore in the end of all the 42 performances. In 1960 a new spex was staged in Göteborg, but "Livet" stayed as an encore in the end of each performance. And so it continued. Now, more than 50 years later it is still a solid tradition to sing this snapsvisa at each Chalmers' spex performance, in Göteborg or on tour, all over Sweden or abroad. The song has been translated to English and German. It is the snapsvisa number one at every party at Chalmers or at all 16 Chalmers Alumni organizations in Sweden and all over the world. It is included in most snaps songbooks printed in Sweden and in Finland, as well as on the Internet.

"Livet är härligt" was included in the third act of the spex, where Katarina's three lovers — Potemkin, Saltykov and Poniatovski, plus farmer Tjoglokov — sing it, proposing a toast for Katarina. The Russian melody is "Poljoschko-pole," which means meadow. It was written in 1934 by Lev Knipper (1898-1975) as part of his fourth symphony "A Song About a Soldier." During wartime, Lev Knipper got recruited by the Cheka, the new Soviet secret police. His sister was movie star Olga Tjekova who made a dazzling career in Nazi Germany keeping company with Hitler and all the Nazi leaders. She made more than 100 German movies between 1921 and 1945, and during this time she was a Soviet spy, enlisted by Lev Knipper.

A newspaper reviewed opening night, reporting: "The snaps song would have the vodka stuck in a Soviet attaché's throat, written as it is to the melody of a communistic camp song." Another paper wrote: "After the singing of 'Livet är härligt' — to the degree that everyone in the audience got thirsty — a toast to the Russian navy was proposed: 'Bottoms up!'"

In the 1940s a song "Som en majdag så skön" was composed as a spoof of another song called "Goodtemplarmarch." The song traveled to Finland. There it was found by a visiting Chalmerist, who brought a pretty sober Good Templar back to Chalmers for an anti-sobering process. A second verse was added as well as the motto: "Hyvästi selvä päivä" (Goodbye Sober Day). Thereafter it was used as a snapsvisa with the title "En aldrig förut sjungen sång" in Chalmers' Erik the Fourteenth spex from 1949. It immediately became a hit.

When hosting a group of Swedish technology students from Göteborg on a study tour to Åbo, Finland, what would you do to get them up at 8 a.m. after an intensive night of partying until 5 a.m.?

This did happen; and the students were scheduled for a study visit at a nearby factory. The hosts, students at the Åbo Academy, found a solution.

The Swedes were all deeply asleep in the dormitory. The hosts first shook them awake, then poured snaps in the jaws of them all — without a snaps song — until they sat bolt upright on their mattresses, gasping for breath and startled out of their sleep, but very soon completely awake and surprisingly quickly ready for their study visit.

What makes a Snapsvisa?

What are the characteristics of a good snapsvisa? There are four important components.

❶ First, and most important: It must be written to a well-known melody so everyone can sing along — no sheet music should be necessary. It takes too long to learn a new melody, and not everyone reads music. Besides, licenses for the printing of music must be obtained from a publisher if the composer died fewer than 70 years ago. Even more complicated is that some music companies, especially American, do not allow alternate texts with melodies. In Sweden, it is generally easier to get a license for printing a snaps song text because it ranks as a folksong. The authors of snaps songs, as well as folk songs, are often anonymous and the texts are considered public property.

Even if the author is known, copyright is almost never discussed because the author of a great snapsvisa will want to spread it as much as possible. As well-known Finnish snaps songwriter Bosse Österberg puts it: "As an author of a snaps song, the finest you can think of is when it lives on by its own. Snaps songs are in the same category as folk songs and you are allowed to use the texts for free without any license."

Keep in mind the tradition of singing snapsvisor is Swedish. Consequently, most melodies are Swedish and not very well known outside Sweden. Most popular melodies are children's songs, folk songs, Bellman songs and "visor" by popular songwriters such as Evert Taube and Povel Ramel.

The most popular Swedish melodies used in the writing of snaps songs are from childrens' songs (such as Mors lilla Olle, Bä, bä, vita lamm, En sockerbagare, Imse vimse spindel och Blinka lilla stjärna där), folk songs (such as Skära, skära havre, Väva vadmal, Höga berg och djupa dalar, Jänta och ja och Månen vandrar sin tysta ban), and older melodies such as Petter Jönsson, Gubben Noak, Kors på Idas grav, Vi gå över daggstänkta berg, Amanda Lundbom, Byssan lull och Hej tomtegubbar.

Many of these older melodies would have long since been forgotten if it was not for their use in snaps songs!

But snaps song melodies have also been imported. For example, J.S. Bach has lent out music, as has Franz Lehàr, Franz Schubert, W.A. Mozart and many other composers of classical music. Lyrics are also sometimes written to music from Great

Britain and the United States, such as Lambeth Walk, When the Saints, You Are My Sunshine, It's a Long Way To Tipperary, Sailor's Hornpipe, Jingle Bells, Oh Susanna, Popeye the Sailor Man, Over the Mountains and Polly Wolly Doodle.

❷ Secondly, a good snapsvisa must be funny, preferably including a joke or some fun that makes it interesting. The lines should be put into rhyme — the funnier the rhymes, the better the snaps song. Four rhymed lines to an easy melody is perfect, for instance this snapsvisa is sung to the very well known melody "Petter Jönsson":

> *Den lilla halvan kan inte göra nån skada,*
> *den brukar bara att något öka vår svada,*
> *den bidrar även till att göra ansikten glada.*
> *Så krök på armen och låt den jäkeln få bada!*

> *The little second can't do much harm,*
> *he usually just increases volubility,*
> *he also contributes to create happy faces.*
> *So, bend your arm and let the bastard bathe!*

❸ A good snapsvisa must be easy to memorize so you'll remember it and sing it at next party.

❹ It must be short. No one wants to sing a long song, while the snaps sits there on the table, waiting. Remember you have to sing before you drink! Snaps song authors knew a long time ago that singers like short and vigorous snaps songs. This one is from a village named Hög, in the province of Hälsingland:

> *Slå i, slå i, bara ideligen,*
> *bara ideligen,*
> *brännvin!*

> *Pour, pour, just continually,*
> *just continually,*
> *snaps!*

Or:

> *Ser du stjärnan i det blå?*
> *Nej!*

> *Do you see the star in the sky?*
> *No!*

When it comes to the brevity of snaps songs, the Finns are the worst. From Sweden's brother nation in the east comes this one:

Icke nu!
Nuuu!

Not now!
Now!

Or, if you want to save even more time and drink your snaps as soon as possible:

Nuuuuu!!!

Now!!!

Ideally, snaps songs should be about something that has to do with drinking or the snaps itself. But the imagination is fertile. Animals are often subjects in snapsvisor:In 1909 people sang about fish; in 1925 people in Finland sang about goats and cattle while the Swedes sang about oxen and cows. In the 1930s came a song about a gull and in the 1940s a song about a camel. Here are more examples of snaps song topics: elephants, fish, geese, cuckoos and all kind of animals, waffles, caviar and a lot of foods, hairy legs and all possible body parts, gastric ulcers and other diseases, a tie in the butter, pee in bed(!), nude girls, archbishops and politics. There is no end to the ingenuity. A snapsvisa can also be about a historic person, such as the following. It also exemplifies a modern kind of snapsvisor that is funny, absurd and has no direct connection with snaps (but is hinting at the results of drinking snaps):

Van Gogh
(Mel: Brevet till Lillan, by Evert Taube)
Stackars van Gogh,
tänk så illa det kan gå,
skar av sej örat
som vi vill bli på.[1]

Poor van Gogh,
how bad it can be,
he cut off his ear
which we'd like to be at.

Or a snapsvisa can describe the feelings when the party is over:

Festen är slut

(Mel: Nu är glada julen slut, slut, slut)

Nu är goda spriten slut, slut, slut.
Alla flaskor har tatts ut, ut, ut.
Inga snapsar mer får tas,
vi har bara tomma glas.
Det är inte roligt!

Now the nice booze is gone, gone, gone.
All the bottles are removed.
We'll have no more snaps to take,
we just have empty glasses.
That's no fun!

Very early on, the type of alcohol became a subject for snapsvisor. Crambamboli was a famous liqueur from Gdansk, Germany and was included in a snapsvisa printed in Germany in 1745. It came to Sweden in the 1800s. Almost any kind of spirits can be found in the texts. It is like reading in a price list from Systembolaget[2]: Renat, Absolut, Kron, OP, Bäsk, Smirnoff, Stoli, Crème de Menthe, Svarta Vinbärs, Ålborgs, Eau-de-vie, Cederlunds, Platins Punsch, Grönstedts Blå, Carlshamns Flagg, Klosterlikör, Bayerskt öl, Whisky, Invalid Port, Koskenkorva, Akvavit, Champagne, Genever, Gin, Guinness, Skåne, Pilsner, Porter, Porsbrännvin, Kumminbrännvin, Konjak, Rhenvin.

1... No direct translation, but "Bli på örat" - literally to become at the ear - means "get drunk."

2... Systembolaget is the government owned chain of liquor stores in Sweden. It is the only retail store allowed to sell alcohol that contains more than 3.5% alcohol (by volume). They carry 80 different varieties of snaps, 250 kinds of beer and a lot of wine (as of 2012).

Collections & Competitions

The Museum of Spirits (Spritmuseum), formerly Vin- & Sprithistoriska Museet in Stockholm, started to collect drinking songs in 1992. The result is a database that now includes almost 10,000 songs, and that number is constantly increasing.

Since 1995 the museum has selected the Swedish Champion of the Year of writing new snaps songs. More than 200 entries are being sent in every year. The ten who proceed to the final must turn up personally to sing their song. The jury likes songs that are easy to sing and are written to a well-known melody.

The Swedish Champion in 2011 was Annika Rymark from Västerås with the following song:

Kräftans tröst
(Mel: I Apladalen)
En liten kräfta sa till sin syster:
Min vän, var inte så svart och dyster.
När du blir stor blir du röd och fin
och du får bada i brännevin.

A little crawfish told his sister:
My friend, don't be that black and gloomy.
When you grow up you'll be red and pretty
and you'll bathe in snaps.

In 2012 the winner was Ulf Söderqvist from Malmö, with:

Börsras
(Mel: Trollkarlen från Indialand or Skånska slott och herresäten)
När börsen har rasat får många panik
för borta är drömmen att bli ack så rik.
Men nubben står stadig som ingenting hänt.
För den ligger alltid kring 40 procent.

When the stock exchange is down much panic breaks out
because the dream to become rich is gone.
But the snaps stays steady as if nothing has happened.
Because it is always about 40 percent.

3... www.spritmuseum.se

Since 2001 Sweden and Finland have competed in the art of writing a new snaps song. The five best from the Swedish Championship then compete with five Finnish entries. This particular competition is always very exciting. The participants compete individually and in teams. Then there is also the audience's choice. In 2011 Sweden won the prize as well as the audience's best choice award. First prize was:

Snille och snaps
(Mel: Petter Jönsson)

Det finns folk vet ni som är intelligenta
och har geniknölar, där man minst kunde vänta!
Vi, som får finnar𝕀 när vi har festat, kan hoppas
att det är brännvinet som får snillet att knoppas!

There are people, you know, who are intelligent
and have brain cudgels where you'll expect it the least!
Us, who get pimples when we partied, can hope
that it is the snaps that makes the genius bud!

In 2012 the Swedish team won again. First prize was:

Tur och retur
(Mel: Litet bo jag sätta vill)

Supen gick i vänster ben,
men med hjälp utav en ven
rusar den tillbaks till knoppen.
För så vist fungerar kroppen,
att ett glas med alkohol
ändå alltid når sitt mål.

The snaps went to the left leg,
but with the help from a vein
it rushes back to the nob.
Because the body works that wisely
that a glass of alcohol
nevertheless always reaches its destination.

𝕀... Finne in Swedish means "pimple" as as "a Finn."

Other snaps song contests

In Atlanta, GA, a new tradition was started in 2011 — a tradition in writing the best Swedish style snaps song, in English. The winners received a bottle of Absolut Vodka. The first year had only four entries, but the second year became a great success with 17 entries. Who knows, maybe this could eventually lead to a Swedish-American Schnapps Song Championship? A great interest in creating new snaps songs has already begun, and the first prize in 2012 went to Anita Menegay for this clever and modern snapsvisa:

Apps & Schnapps
(Mel: Auld Land Syne)

In this new modern world of ours
there are a lot of apps.
But none of them can take the place
of a good old fashioned snaps.

Second prize also turned out to be Anita Menegay. This is a longer song, but to a rhythmic and inspiring melody:

Papa Loves Vodka
(Mel: Papa Loves Mambo)

Papa loves Vodka,
papa loves Vodka.
Mama loves Vodka,
mama loves Vodka.
Look at'em sniffing it,
look at'em sipping it,
look at'em swilling it, yes!

Papa loves Vodka,
tra la la la la.
Mama loves Vodka,
tra la la la la.
Look at'em stay with it,
look at'em play with it,
look at'em sway with it yes! Olé!

He drinks up, she falls down.
He weaves left, she crawls right.

Papa's looking for Mama,
but Mama's nowhere in sight!
Papa loves Vodka....

The third place winner was Jan Rygert, with this song that includes a built-in call for the opening of another bottle.

Get Your Glasses
(Mel: Frère Jacques)

Get your glasses, get the vodka,
fill them high
to the sky.
Put a little booze in, put a little spice in.
Drink it fast.
Make it last.

Create Your Own Snapsvisa

There aren't really any rules for how to write a snapsvisa or a drinking song. However, if you want to create something that will have a chance to survive past the party you are writing it for, or if you want to submit it to a snaps song competition, there are a few suggestions for what to do and not do (also see "What makes a Snapsvisa," on page 43).

DO find a melody that is well known, especially to the people attending the party at which you will present the song. If you want your song to survive, it is important that it is either a very well known Swedish melody or a melody that is well known in the United States as well as in Sweden.

DO rhyme the lines! It makes the song easier to remember and more pleasant to sing. The funnier the rhymes, the better.

DO write about a particular subject. You can write about how to drink, how to digest, how to behave, how to do this and that, what to drink (it must be about snaps — however it is generally better to not mention any specific kind of drink).

DO be funny. Most important is that the text is funny and at least somewhat related to drinking snaps. The best and most jury-appreciated — if you will be participating in a snaps song contest — is if the song has a joke or something funny in the end.

DO reach out. If you want to give your song a chance to survive to a wider circle you would need to take these steps:

❶ Make sure your song is included on the song-sheet that will be handed out at the dinner party or celebration that you write it for.

❷ Get your song posted on websites, Facebook, etc.

❸ Provide your song to editors of snaps song websites. On some websites you can post your song yourself.

❹ Try to get your song included in new snaps songbooks. Send the song to editors.

❺ Participate in Spritmuseum's annual snaps song contest. (See page 56 and 98)

DO NOT write about whisky and wine if you are writing a snapsvisa. A snapsvisa must be about snaps, drunk from snaps glasses — if you even need to mention a beverage at all.

DO NOT write a song that is long or has many verses. As previously said, you want to drink your snaps as soon as possible! Four lines make a perfect snapsvisa, eight lines are OK, more than that is not recommended.

Short snaps songs may take a long time to create. One of the authors of "Korta Solen" from 1971 tells us about all the difficulties behind the writing of this song: "According to notes in our guest book, it happened on Friday May 7, 1971 that my friend and I were walking at the tarn at Änggårdsbergen. The old saying 'Ordning och reda — lövning på freda' (Order and method — confusion on Friday) became applicable because as we were there it became time for defoliation, specially from bog-myrtle.[1]) We started collecting and after hard work and some time we became "bladiga."[2]) Eventually it was time to go home to get herring, chives and new potatoes on our balcony. Exhilarated and in good spirits we thought we finally had to create a song. But first we had to invent "Nya Gårnerklubben" (The New Gårner Club). After the song eventually was created we first basooned it out for a number of totally uninterested children, then for our wives, who all were fairly newly wed. Then we made assiduous efforts in the honoring of our new composition. The song spread and has even been translated to foreign lingos."

Korta Solen
(Mel: The authors' own composition)
Solen går upp och ner,
och snapsen går ner.

The sun goes up and down,
And the snaps goes down.

1... Bog-myrtle is excellent for spicing of snaps.
2... "Bladig" means "like a leaf" but also "somewhat intoxicated."

How to liven up parties

There are many ways of livening up parties. The best of them all is, of course, the singing of snapsvisor. The most bizarre was in 1960 when a student at Chalmers got it into his head that it would be terrifically amusing for the party go-ers to spend the evening with a cow. The student had connections in the country, so he persuaded his friend the farmer to pry the cow onto his truck and carry her to the festival premises before the arrival of the party participants. A corner was claimed for the cow, with straw and hay:

> The moo-cow was invited, however slightly surprised.
> The dinner guests arrived, considerably more surprised.
> A snaps song was executed.
> The cow mooed, however in the wrong key.
> The snaps was taken. The cow ate her hay.
> The appetizer was eaten. The cow peed.
> The main course was served. The cow shit.

At this point the participants either choked or had to drink all the available booze in order to alleviate their senses of smell. People chose to retire from the party. So did the cow, who accepted the rejection with a resounding moo. The stench took a long time to get rid of. In fact, the small, old party building in which this happened had to be demolished not long thereafter. The connection between the incident and the demolition was however never determined.

Drinking Rules & Motto

The snaps songs and the drinking of snaps must be followed by some drinking rules. That is a decree by Finnish snaps song author Bosse Österberg. His rules are as follows.

! The one who does not eat fish must not have a snaps.

! All foods count as fish except for pancakes and cheese.

! The one who eats cheese may be allowed to drink from his fish-eating neighbor's glass.

! If everyone eats cheese, then also cheese counts as fish.

! Pancakes follow the same rule as cheese.

And this somewhat confusing "motto" was found in a snaps songbook from 1973:

> One snaps is no snaps.
> Two snapses are half-a-snaps.
> Two half snapses are one snaps.
> Two whole snapses are one church snaps.
> Two church snapses are one crown snaps.

A crown snaps ("kronsup") was a large snaps of one "kvarter," that is 8.175 cl or 2.7 fluid ounces. It is mentioned in Bellman's Fredmans Epistel #17.

A church snaps ("kyrksup") was a snaps (in the 19th century and probably earlier) that was imbibed by the priest and men (no women!) present at the dinner following Sunday's service.

Snaps songs and women

Someone wrote:

> Nubben är en form av spriten,
> varav damer få en liten.
> The snaps is a form of alcohol,
> of which ladies [only] get a little one.

From Christina Mattsson's book "Från Helan till lilla Manasse" the following is taken:

> Admiral Carl Tersmeden described in his memoirs how in 1735
> drinking-bouts in upper-class environments were arranged, with
> no other purpose than the drinking. There were women around the

table, drinking moderately. Tersmeden said: "The madams helped me while I in one draught emptied half-a-bouteille while the ladies just sipped from the goblet." He also described how the gentlemen drank like men but the girls had to sing, so they always got a full thank-you glass from the men.

In the end of the 19th century, Swedish author Marika Stiernstedt wrote about middle-class life in Stockholm. She wrote that she never heard they sang to the snaps — at least not when ladies were present. And the ladies were not supposed to drink alcohol. A lady never had anything stronger than wine. The most scandalous thing you could hear about a lady was that she was sipping wine at home alone. And having a snaps at a dinner party with the men was completely out of the question.

Not even among students in university cities 100 years ago was it natural for women. The history of students' singing is the history of men's singing. As late as in the 1930s, the male students in Sweden still preferred to gather at parties "around Bacchi" without ladies. At singing tours, frequently arranged by students, they brought snaps songs. But participating women were not allowed to join the supper ("sexa") when snaps was served. In a report from a singing tour to Paris, France, in 1878, it was pointed out that ladies did participate at the dinner, but in an adjacent room, and that this presence of the women was a serious breach of etiquette: "To have supper (sexa) has, from time immemorial, been one of the most sacred privileges of the sterner sex."

Snaps and Sex

This chapter is short, for the reason that it is difficult to do these two things at the same time. A waste in every way if attempted.

If you insist to learn more about the subject, check out a number of more or less finely tuned snaps songs in collections of snapsvisor on the Internet. Many have chapters called "Fula visor" (Dirty Songs).

Do not be confused by the song "Sexten" and its words "Sex, sex, vi vill ha sex." It is not what you think. It means "Six, six, we wantNo. six."

Spritakademien

In 2012 the Swedish Spritakademien (Academy of Spirits) started. It will promote and develop the classical culture of spirits in Sweden.

The members are:

Chair No. 1... Steffo Törnquist, president, author, member of the Board of Directors of Spritmuseum

Chair No. 2... Angela D'Orazio, master blender at Mackmyra, Swedish whisky producer

Chair No. 3... Jonas Odland, spice master

Chair No. 4... Eric Berntsson, snaps producer

Chair No. 5... Göran Lundqvist, president of Spritmuseum, former SEO of Absolut Vodka

Chair No. 6... Eva Lennman, curator at Spritmuseum

Chair No. 7... Stefano Catenacci, chef at Operakällaren, Stockholm, which is purveyor to His Majesty the King

Chair No. 8... Solveigh Sommarström, chemist, teacher, snaps producer

Chair No. 9... Per Hermansson, snaps sensory specialist

Chair No. 10... Rolf Cassegren, President of the Sprit och Vin Suppliers

Chair No. 11... Ernst Billgren, artist

Chair No. 12... Louise Hoffsten, singer

Chair No. 13... Hasse Nilsson, author

Chair No. 14... Carl Frosterud, Sommelier

Snapses - Order of priority

There is a name for every snaps you drink at a party. That's an old tradition in Sweden — its origin in the present form is from universities.

"Helan" (#1), "Halvan" (#2) and "Tersen" (#3) are the most well known. Even in Svenska Akademins Ordlista (The Swedish Academy's Wordlist) you will find that "Ters" means "Tredje supen" (The third snaps).

The origin of "Helan" and "Halvan" is from a song manuscript from 1760. The smallest measure for liquids by then was "halvjumfru" (half maid), equal to 4.1 cl (about 1.4 fluid ounces). The text in the song was:

Gjut brännvin i din strupa
half Jungfru eller hel
eller ideliga supa.

Pour snaps down your throat
half Jungfru or whole
or continually drink.

The first time "Helan" was used in a snaps song was early in the 19th century. "Halvan" (Hur länge skall) was written in the 1870s and "Tersen" in the 1940s or '50s.

More and more names have since been added. In 1950 about 14 snapsar were named. In 2000 the number grew to 20.

Here is the list:
1 Helan = The First (literally, "the whole")
2 Halvan = The Second (literally, "the half")
3 Tersen = The Third
4 Kvarten = The Fourth
5 Kvinten = The Fifth
6 Rivan = Has to do with the word "riva" » "rasp", "burn."
The word does NOT mean The Sixth!
7 Septen = The Seventh
8 Rafflan = Has to do with the word "raffel" » "thriller"; at Lund's University the word "Okten" for the eigth was used.
9 Rännan = Has to do with the word "ränna" » "trench", "drain" or maybe running (also "ränna")
10 Smuttan = The sip
11 Smuttans unge = The sip's baby
12 Smuttans andra unge = The sip's second baby
13 Femton droppar = Fifteen drops
14 Lilla Manasse = Manasse was a king who ruled in Judah from about 696 to 642 B.C. He was described as an apostate, who abandoned the right belief in God.
15 Lilla Manasses broder = Little Manasse's brother
16 Lilla Manasses brylling = Little Manasse's third cousin
17 Finalen = The final
18 Kreaturens återuppståndelse = The resurrection of creatures
19 Den bleka dödens dryck = The drink of the pallid Death
20 Sista spiken = The last nail

Snapsvisor in Swedish

Snaps songs come and go. Some live a longer life and some become classics. In older times they lived by oral tradition only. Now they live thanks to numerous snaps songbooks, produced by students, organizations, celebrities and others. Only at Chalmers were 60 to 70 snaps songbooks printed between 1936 and 2007. And that does not include all song sheets and snaps song booklets produced for banquets and special events.

You can find almost everything you are looking for on the Internet. If you google the word "Snapsvisa" you'll get 163,000 results, of which many are sheer snaps song libraries. One of the sites has about 900 different snaps songs. All are in Swedish.

Very few Swedish snaps songs have been translated to English. Sometimes it is difficult to make a close translation because the character of the song can easily get lost. There are many Swedish words, sentences and meanings that cannot be closely — or at all — translated.

Here follows 26 of the most well known evergreens, classic or snaps song standards in Swedish. Each is provided with a word for word translation.

These songs are however not singable in their English translation. This is because we want you to understand the original meaning of the songs without all the circumlocutions that are often necessary to provide meter and rhymes when you try to translate to English. Some of the context may get lost.

Byssan lull

(Mel: Byssan lull)
The song was written for a banquet at Chalmers, Göteborg, in 1958. It is widely spread on the Internet. The author was the same as the author of this book.

Byssan lull, utav brännvin blir man full,
slipsen man doppar i smöret.
Och näsan den blir röd,
och ögonen får glöd,
men tusan så bra blir humöret!

[Byssan lull], the snaps will make you tipsy,
you'll dip the tie in the butter.
And the nose will get red,
and the eyes will glow,
but your spirits will be damned good!

Du ska få mitt gamla snapsglas

(Mel: He'll Be Coming Round the Mountains)
The Swedish Champion in the writing of new snaps songs in 2007 was Erik de Maré from Malmö. This was his winning song in the competition with 200 other entries.

Du ska få mitt gamla snapsglas när jag dör.

Du ska få mitt gamla snapsglas när jag dör.

När jag reser mig ur askan

dricker jag direkt ur flaskan.

Du ska få mitt gamla snapsglas när jag dör.

En droppe vatten

(Mel: Petter Jönsson)
The "Petter Jönsson" melody is one of the most used by snaps songwriters. It is a chapbook song from 1870 about a Swedish emigrant's problem when he went to America.

En droppe vatten kan inte läska en tunga.

En nypa luft kan ej heller fylla en lunga.

En ensam ko räcker inte till för att kalva.

En stackars Hela behöver också en Halva.

A drop of water is not enough to refresh a tongue.

A breath of air cannot fill a lung.

A longely cow is not enough to make calves.

A poor First will also need a Second.

Fordom odlade man vindruvsranka

(Mel: Vintern rasat ut)
The song was included in a snaps songbook called Nubbevisor, *in 1945.*

Fordom odlade man vindruvsranka

ur vars frukt man gjorde ädelt vin.

Nu man pressar saften ur en planka,

doftande av äkta terpentin.

Höj din bägare, oh broder yster

och låt friska skogen glida kall

nerför strupen, och om du är dyster

låt oss supa upp en liten tall.

Formerly they cultivated grapes

from which they produced noble wine.

Now they press the juice from a plank

that smells from genuine turpentine.

Raise your globet, oh frisky brother,
and let the fresh woods slide cold
down that throat, and if you are gloomy
let's drink away a small pine-tree.

För att mänskan ska

(Mel: Bä, bä, vita lamm)
First time this text was published was in 1945, in Chalmers sångbok.

För att mänskan ska trivas på vår jord
fordras att hon har på sitt smörgåsbord
en stor, stor sup åt far,
en liten sup åt mor
och två små droppar åt lille, lille bror.

For man to thrive on our earth
he needs upon his smörgåsbord
a large, large drink for father,
a little drink for mother
and two small drops for the little, little brother.

Första supen är redan nerklämd

(Mel: Höga berg och djupa dalar)
This is a song to Halvan. It was probably written in the 1960s.

Första supen är redan nerklämd,
sången klingar allt mera flerstämd.
Hej hopp, min lilla halva sup,
du ska ut för ett hemskt och gräsligt stup!
//: Hej där försvann den –
och kvar är blott ett glas i handen. ://

The first snaps has already been gulped down,
the singing sounds more and more polyphonic.
Hey hop, you my little half snaps
you are going down a ghastly and terrible slope!
//: Hey, there it went –
and left behind is just a glass in my hand. ://

HEJ TOMTEGUBBAR

Melodi: Hej, tomtegubbar.
Melodin till denna visa publicerades första gången 1815. Då fanns ingen text — den kom senare under 1800-talet. Som skålvisa är den använd sedan början av 1900-talet.

Hej, tom - te - gub - bar, slå i gla - sen och låt oss lus - ti - ga va - ra. va - ra. En li - ten tid vi le - va här med myck - en mö - da och stort be - svär. Hej, tom - te - gub - bar, slå i gla - sen och låt oss lus - ti - ga va - ra!

Hej, tomtegubbar

(Mel: Original)
This is one of the oldest snaps songs still very much alive. Actually it is mandatory singing every Christmas, with or without a snaps. It is also one of the songs you sing when you dance around the Christmas tree. The text is from the 19th century. The melody is even older, it was printed in 1815.

//: Hej tomtegubbar[1], slå i glasen
och låt oss lustiga vara. ://
En liten tid, vi leva här
med mycken möda och stort besvär.
//: Hej tomtegubbar slå i glasen
och låt oss lustiga vara! ://

*//: Hey, all tomte-brownies[1], pour the glasses
and let's have fun. ://
We live here for a short time
with a lot of trouble and great pains.
//: Hey, all tomtegubbars, pour the glasses
and let's have fun. ://*

---

[1]... "Tomte" is a Santa-like elf in Swedish Christmas and God Jul tradition. In this case "tomtegubbar" literally translates to tomte-brownie, where brownies are folkloric house fairies.

Helan kommer, helan går

(Mel: Kovan kommer, kovan går)
An unknown author created this travesty on Emil Norlander's "Kovan kommer, kovan går".
First printed in the snaps song collection Pärlan (The Pearl), 1927.

Helan kommer, helan går,
helan går, helan går.
Halvan följer helans spår,
helans spår, helans spår.
Nubben den får ingen spara,
helan den ska sväljas bara.
Helan kommer, helan går,
Helan comes, helan goes,
lycklig den som helan får.

The First comes, The First goes (down),
The First goes, The First goes.
The Second will follow in The First's footsteps.
The snaps should be saved by no one,
the snaps should only be swallowed.
The First comes, The First goes,
the one who gets The First will be happy.

I Finland djupa skogar

(Mel: Rio-raj-raj)
This snaps song was included in the spex "Sven Duva", in 1965, at Chalmers University of Technology in Göteborg.

I Finlands djupa skogar,
In Finland's deep forests
där får man supa gratis,
you can drink for free,
hej bom faderi, där får man supa gratis.
hey bom faderi, there you can drink for free.
Fast man blandat bark i både vete och potatis,[2]
bom, faderi och faderallan lej!

In Finland's deep forests
you can drink for free,
hey bom faderi, there you can drink for free.
Though, they mixed in bark with the wheat and potato.[2]
Bom, faderi and faderallan ley!

2... As in, they added tree bark to the wheat and potato (akvavit ingredients).

Imbelupet glaset står

(Mel: Kors på Idas grav)

One of the most beloved snaps songs of the 20th century is this one from the 1920s. It is a travesty of the chapbook song "Kors på Idas grav", that begins with "Mossbelupen hydda står vid Heklas fot" The snaps song was printed first time in Nylänningarnas sångbok, Helsinki, *in 1925.*

Imbelupet glaset står på bräcklig fot,
kalla pilsnerflaskor luta sig därmot.
Men därnere, miserere,
uti magens dunkla djup
sitter djävulen och väntar på en sup.

The misted over glass is standing on a brittle foot,
cold lager bottles are leaning against it.
But down there, miserere,
in my stomache's obscure depth
sits the devil, waiting for a snaps.

Jag hade en snaps en gång

(Mel: Jag hade en gång en båt (C. Vreeswijk))

Jag hade en snaps en gång,
jag hörde en ton slås an.
Så sjöng vi en liten sång
och snapsen försvann!
Svara mej du: Var är den nu?
Jag bara undrar: Var är den nu?

Once I had a snaps,
I heard a tone strike.
Then we sang a little song
and the snaps disappeared!
Answer me: Where is it now?
I just wonder: Where is it now.

Krök armen i vinkel

(Mel: Väva vadmal)

Tore Pekka Norén, a student from KTH (The Royal Institute of Technology), Stockholm wrote this one in the 1940s. The third line of the text is just a transposition of letters.

Krök armen i vinkel.

Här vankas det finkel

Och fika vankel och vanka finkel

och kröka armen i vinkel.

Bend your arm in an angle.

There will be fusel.

[And fere be thusel and willa fusel]

and bending your arm in an angle.

Livet är härligt

(Mel: Stepnaya Kavaleriskaya)

Since the 1960s this snaps song has been one of the most popular and it has kept its popularity over the years. Its origin is the "Chalmersspexet" at Chalmers' University of Technology in Göteborg. It was included in the spex "Katarina II", in 1959.

//: Livet är härligt,

tavarich, vårt liv är härligt.

Vi alla våra små bekymmer glömmer

när vi har fått en tår på tand, en skål!

Ta dej en vodka,

tavarich, en liten vodka.

Glasen i botten vi tillsammans tömmer,

det kommer mera efter hand. ://

Hej!

Långt ner i Småland

(Mel: Trad.)

The oldest evidence of this song is from a hand-written music-book belonging to Östgöta Nation at the University of Uppsala, dated 1889-1890. The chorus "Hurra för Svealand" was used by August Strindberg in his book Hemsöborna, 1887. His refrain was: "Hurra för Svealand! Hurra för Nederland! Hurra för oss alla, nu tar vi oss en dram!"

Långt ner i Småland där rider själva djävulen

med laddade pistoler och knallande gevär.

Och alla små djävlar, de spela på fioler,

och själva fader satan, han spelar handklaver.

Hurra för Götaland,

hurra för Svealand,

hurra för potatisland som ger oss brännevin.

Far down in Småland where the devil himself rides
with loaded pistols and blazing guns.
And all small devils, they play the violin
and father Satan himself, he plays the accordion.
Hurrah for Götland,
hurrah for Svealand,
hurrah for the potato field that gives us snaps.

Min lilla lön

(Mel: Hej tomtegubbar)
This snaps song was recorded in 1931 by Swedish entertainer and actor Sigge Fürst and was printed in many snaps songbooks in the 1930s.

Min lilla lön den räcker inte,
den går till öl och till brännvin.
Till öl och brännvin går den åt
och lite flickor emellanåt.
Min lilla lön den räcker inte,
den går till öl och till brännvin.

My small salary is not enough,
it goes to beer and brandy.
To beer and brandy it goes
and a little, occassionaly, for girls.
My small salary is not enough,
it goes to beer and brandy.

Måsen

(Mel: När månen vandrar)
This is one of the most well known Swedish snaps songs. It can be traced to the 1930s, to a snaps songbook called Bellmansro Nubbevisor. *The text alludes to a commercial from the turn of the century for "OP Andersson Akvavit".*

Det satt en mås på en klyvarbom,
och tom i krävan var kräket.
Och tungan lådde vid skepparns gom
där han satt uti bleket.
Jag vill ha sill, hördes måsen rope,
och skepparn svarte: Jag vill ha OP,
om blott jag får, om blott jag får.

There sat a seagull on a jibboom
And an empty craw he held.
A skipper's tongue stuck to his palate,
there he sat quite pale.
I want herring, the gull was heard crying,
and the skipper answered: I want OP,
if only I may, if only I may.

När helan man tagit
(Mel: Skånska slott och herresäten)

This snaps song from the 1950s – or even earlier – is still very much alive. The original text to this melody is, however, long forgotten. The melody has survived through this text, and other snaps songs to the same melody.

När helan man tagit och halvan ska dricka,
det är som att kyssa en nymornad flicka.
Ju mera man får, desto mer vill man ha.
En ensammer jäkel gör alls ingen gla'.

When you had The First and are drinking The Second,
it's like kissing a newly awakened girl.
The more you get, the more you want.
A lonely devil will make no one happier.

Punschen kommer
(Mel: Lehár's well-known waltz from "The Merry Widow")

This homage to the punsch was written by a student at KTH (The Royal Institute of Technology, Stockholm) in 1942. He wrote it for a competition called "Sångartävlan." The punsch is unique for Sweden – and at one point you could only get it in Sweden. The main ingredient is arrack, made from fermented fruit, grain and sugarcane. The arrack was imported from Egypt in the 18th century. 100 years later Swedes started to make punsch, and very soon someone found out that the combination of pea soup and punsch was excellent, especially with warm punsch. This yellow drink came to be extremely popular at Swedish universities and colleges. One snaps songbook explains that "Punsch should be drunk either very cold with dessert, any day of the week, or hot with peasoup on Thursdays."

Punschen kommer, punschen kommer,
ljuv och sval.
Glasen imma, röster stimma
i vår sal.
Skål för glada minnen,
skål för varje vår.
Inga sorger finnas mer när punsch vi får.

The punsch is here, the punsch is here,
sweet and cool.
The glasses are misting, the voices growing
in our hall.
Toast for happy memories,
toast to each spring.
There will be no more sorrow when we get the punsch.

Till supen så tager man sill

(Mel: Vi gå över daggstänkta berg)
Also called "Smuttan," the tenth snaps in the order of priority (see page 56).
It is from the 1920s.

Till supen så tager man sill, sill, sill,

men också ansjovis om man så vill, vill, vill.

Och om man är oviss,

om sillen är ansjovis,

så tar man bara några supar till, till, till.

With the drinks you take herring, herring, herring,
but also achovies if you like, like, like.
And if you are uncertain,
if the herring is anchovy,
then take a few drinks more, more, more.

Tomma glas i gott kalas

(Mel: Original)
Frans Michael Franzén (1772-1847) was a bishop in the Swedish city of Härnösand. He wrote
several snaps songs and this is one of them. It was printed in 1824 in Trenne muntra
sällskaps-wisor.

Tomma glas i gott kalas
värden icke hedra.
Därför fyller jag mitt glas,
bröder, fyllen edra!

Fulla glas i gott kalas
gästerna ej hedra.
Därför tömmer jag mitt glas,
bröder, tömmen edra!

Empty glasses at a good party
are not esteemed by the host.
Therefore, I fill my glas,
brothers, fill yours!

Full glasses at a good party
are not esteemed by guests.
Therefore, I empty my glass,
brothers, empty yours!

Tänk om jag hade lilla nubben

(Mel: Hej tomtegubbar)
"Hej tomtegubbar" from 1815 is, at Christmas, one of the most popular songs in Sweden. It is
also a popular melody for snaps songs. This text is from the 1950s.

//: Tänk om jag hade lilla nubben
på ett snöre i halsen. ://
Och kunde dra den upp och ner,
så att den kändes som många fler.
Tänk om jag hade lilla nubben
på ett snöre i halsen.

//: What if I had a little snaps
on a string in my throat. ://
And could pull it up and down
so it felt as if there were many more.
What if I had a little snaps
on a string in my throat.

Törsten rasar

(Mel: Vintern rasat ut)
The song was included in a snaps songbook from 1929, called Motbok 1929. Since then many
variations of these original words have been composed and printed.

Törsten rasar uti våra strupar.
Tungan hänger torr och styv och stel.
Men snart vankas stora, långa supar,
var och en får sin beskärda del.
Snapsen kommer, den vill vi tömma,
denna nektar, likt Olympens saft,
kommer oss att våra sorger glömma.
Snapsen skänker hälsa, liv och kraft.

The thirst rages in our throats.
The tongue hangs dry and stiff and rigid.
But soon we'll be treated to a large, long drink,
and everyone will get their share.
The snaps is coming, we want to empty it,
this nectar, like Olympus' juice,
will make us forget our sorrows.
The snaps gives us health, life and power.

Utan smärta

(Mel: Gubben Noak)
It is believed that this snaps song was written by a student at KTH in the 1940s.

Utan smärta, till vårt hjärta
nubben sig begav.
Åkte som på kana,
sån't beror på vana.
Tack du lille att du ville
gå hos oss i kvav.

Painless to our hearts
the snaps departs.
It slides down
due to practice.
Thanks, little one, for wanting
to go down with us.

Uti min mage

(Mel: Uti vår hage)
There are many versions of this snaps song. The oldest known printed version is this one, from 1936.

Uti min mage en längtan mig tär,
kom hjärtansfröjd[1].
Där råder en hunger, som ropar så här:
Kom kryddsill och kall potatis,
kom brännvin och *quantum satis*[2],
kom allt som kan drickas,
kom hjärtansfröjd[1].

1... Hjärtansfröjd, literally translated, is "heart's joy". It is an herb used both medicinally and for flavor.
2... Borrowed latin meaning "the amount which is needed."

A craving wrenches at my stomach.
Come, lemon balm[1].
There is a hunger that cries so:
come, pickled herring and cold potatoes;
come, snaps and quantum satis[2];
come, all that is drinkable;
come, lemon balm[1].

Å sella ho går i havet
(Mel: Och jungfrun hon går i ringen)
This snaps song most likely emanates from Sweden's west coast, written on a dialect from that region. First time it was printed was in Chalmers sångbok *in 1950.*

//: Å sella ho går i havet
bland torsk å makrill. ://
//: Ho mår inte illa av'et,
ho tar en sup när ho vill. ://

//: In the sea, the herring dwell,
among the cod and mackerel. ://
//:: A piece o' mind, she pays none,
she'll drink when she wants one. ://

Än går det vågor i halvankaren
(Mel: Original)
The song was first printed in Norrland's Nation's songbook at Uppsala University in 1910. The text alludes to the fluid (beer or small beer) in a small keg.

Än går det vågor i halvankaren,
i halvankaren, i halvankaren.
Än går det vågor i halvankaren,
i halvankaren går det vågor än.
Och så rulla vi på kuttingen igen!

There are waves in the keg,
in the keg, in the keg.
There are waves in the keg,
in the keg there are waves.
So, let's roll it again!

Snapsvisor in English

Probably only a fraction of a percent of all Swedish snaps songs have been translated to English. Here is my choice of 25 of them, all singable. The music, as well as more translated songs, can be found in the book *The Very Best of Swedish Schnapps Songs*[¥].

A Mouthful Of Vodka
(Mel: A Spoonful Of Sugar)
Just a mouthful of vodka
will make anything go down,
anything go down,
anything go down.
Just a mouthful of vodka
will make anything go down
in the most delightful way!

A Word From the Snaps
(Mel: Music, Music, Music)
Snifter, Kicker, Hooch or Dram,
-what you call me: Here I am.
Lift me up and pour me down
the whistle, whistle, whistle.
Hey!

Bumble-Bees
(Mel: Popeye the Sailor Man)
We are little bumble-bees, bzz, bzz.
We are little bumble-bees, bzz, bzz.
We are little bumble-bees taking a buzzer.
We are little bumble-bees.
Cheerszz!

Do It My Way
(Mel: Lambeth Walk)
If you drink too few you still are dry.
If you drink too many you can die.
Do it my way:
Take a snapsie ev'ry day!
Hey!

¥... Available from Nordstjernan Förlag at www.nordicsampler.com.

Five Ounces

(Mel: Five Dirty Little Fingers)

Five ounces from the freezer
of some strong and spicy booze.
That makes a pretty teaser
to my tickly little nose.
Maybe I'll have a dinner
with a sandwich and a steak,
if I manage stay awake
after drinking all that booze!

Getting Tipsy In a Bar

(Mel: Twinkle, Twinkle Little Star)

Getting tipsy in a bar,
how I wonder where I are.
Absolut you are my friend,
hanging tight until the end.
Even though I'm on the floor
you're so good I just want more.

I Like the Snaps

(Mel: Over the Mountains)

I like the snaps, the snaps likes me,
thrilling as only a snaps can be.
I want to drink the real elite:
Ålborger Aquavit.
//: Over the mountains, over the sea,
thousands of snapsies are waiting for me.
Please go to hell with juice and tea,
snaps is the drink for me! ://

In My Belly

(Mel: Brother Jacob)

In my belly is a smelly
I don't like. You don't like!
Give me something peptic,
very antiseptic:
Give me booze! Vodka-juice!

I See a Small One
(Mel: Satin Doll)

I see a small one.
Just drink it!
You see a small one.
Just drink it!
(Everyone drinks the snaps)
We sat' em!
We sat' em!
SKÅL!

It's a Long Way
(Mel: It's a Long Way To Tipperary)

It's a long way for little Drammy,
it's a long way to go.
I feel a burning in my tummy,
and it tickles in each toe.
I get tinnitus from a toddy
and a tremor from a nip.
It says: "Ugh, ugh, ugh," there in my body,
but's a wonderful trip!

Life Is a Pleasure
(Mel: Stepnaya Kavaleriskaya)
This song in Swedish: See page 41 and 65.

//: Life is a pleasure,
tavarich, a great, big pleasure.
All our troubles are reduced to zero
when we have got a drop to wet our gum.
Let's have a vodka,
tavarich, a little vodka,
empty your gobbler like a Viking hero,
there will be many more to come. ://
Hey!

Little, Little Vodka
(Mel: Imsy Wimsy Spider)

Little, little Vodka was going down the hatch.
But little Tummy didn't want to catch.
Up came the Vodka, looked around — and then
little, little Vodka went down the hatch again.

Number One a Pleasure Was

(Mel: Oh, Susanna)

Number One a pleasure was to drown,
but my belly wants some more.
Number Two must also now go down
or else you'll hear a roar:
Hey man, listen!
This is what you should know:
Both colitis crap and ulcer spots
disappear from vodka shots!

Oh, When the Schnapps

(Mel: Oh, When the Saints)

Oh, when the Schnapps,
oh, when the Schnapps,
oh, when the Schnapps is marchin' on.
Then I will be there, when he's coming
and let him join crawfish and prawn.

Old Mac Donald

(Mel: Old Mac Donald Had a Farm)

Old Mac Donald had a dram,
E I E I O.
And then he had another two,
E I E I O.
He went hee hee here,
he went haw haw there,
he went hee-haw hee-haw here and there.
Old Mac Donald had a dram,
now let's have one, too!

Schnapps and Beer

(Mel: Jingle Bells)

Schnapps and beer, happy sheer,
let's get in the mood.
Smörgåsbord with lots of food,
friends from far and near.
Gathered here, schnapps so dear,
drink without a fear.
Celebrate! We must not wait.
Schnapps is just too great!

There's a Place In a Bar
(Mel: The Snake Charmer)

There's a place in the bar,
they make Absolut the star.
There's a hole in my face,
where I pour it by the case.

The Swedish Cook
(Mel: Polly Wolly Doodle)

I'm the Swedish Cook, who the pans forsook,
singing hurley burley birdie all the day!
Now I'll undertake
what I won't forsake:
Drinking barely barley brewage all the way!
SKÅL!!!

To Improve Your Appetite
(Mel: California Here I Come)

To improve your appetite
you should take a vodka-bite.
The more you are scoffing
the more you want to get
from Smirnoff or Stoli,
that wouldn't be a bet for you
'cause alcohol is pretty rude,
spec'ally without any food.
But each time we have a fest
Absolut is always best!

What a Vodka
(Mel: Oh, My Darling Clementine)

What a vodka, what a vodka,
it's the smoothest to my throat.
It's the purest and maturest.
It's the famous Absolut!

Twinkle, Twinkle, Vodka Bar
(Mel: Twinkle, Twinkle, Little Star)

Twinkle, twinkle, vodka bar,
how I wonder how you are.
Hope you have a shot for me.
Give me two and give me tree.
Twinkle, twinkle, vodka bar,
soon I'm b'low mahogany!

Vodka, vodka
(Mel: Stenka Rasin)

Vodka, vodka, drink of heaven.
Vodka, vodka, drink of hell.
//: Don't resist any temptation,
soon enough you'll hear the bell! ://

When I Get Drunker
(Mel: When I Get Older)

When I get drunker, loosing my mind
many beers from now.
Will I still be having me a jolly good time,
whisky, gin and a bottle of wine.
So, fill the glasses — drunk as a skunk —
don't say you want more,
cause we are singers,
and we are swingers,
join us and you won't get bored!

You Can Have Another Yet
(Mel: Popeye the Sailor Man)

You can have another yet.
They're nicer the more you get.
But if you have twenty
you'll wake up with plenty
of headache and much regret!

You'll Inherit My Shotglass
(Mel: He'll Be Coming Round the Mountain)
This song in Swedish: See page 60.

//: You'll inherit my old shotglass when I die. ://
When my mortal time elapses
I'll be swigging all my schnappses.
You'll inherit my old shotglass when I die.

Snapsvisor by Swedish Celebrities

Please note that the translations are not singable.

Bordeaux, Bordeaux

(Mel: I sommarens solliga dagar)
Claes Eriksson, writer and leader of the group of entertainers "Galenskaparna" wrote this popular drinking song for a party at Valborgsmässoafton 1973.

Jag minns än idag hur min fader
kom hem ifrån staden så glader
och rada upp flaskor i rader
och sade nöjd som så: "Bordeaux, Bordeaux!"
Han drack ett glas, kom i extas
och sedan blev det stort kalas.
Och vi små glin,
ja vi drack vin
som första klassens fyllesvin.
Och vi dansade runt där på golvet
och skrek så vi blev blå:
"Bordeaux, Bordeaux!"

I still remember how my father
came home from the city very jocular
and lined bottles in a row
and said with satisfaction: "Bordeaux, Bordeaux!"
He drank a glass, went into ecstasy,
upon which there was a great party.
And us, small youngsters,
yes, we drank wine
like first-class boozers.
And we danced there on the floor
and screamed, till we turned blue:
"Bordeaux, Bordeaux!"

Det var en lördags afton

(Mel: Det var en lördagsafton)
By well-known Swedish-Danish musician Mikael Neuman, son of Ulrik Neuman of Swedish-Danish world fame.

//: Det var en lördags aften jeg tog "en lille en." ://

"En lille en," "en lille en," gik ned i mine ben.

Så efter mange "lille en" jeg sov snart som en sten.

/:: It was a Saturday evening and I had "a small one." ://

"A small one," "a small one," went to the bone.

After many "a small one" I slept like a stone.

Gamla gubbar

(Mel: I Apladalen i Värnamo)
This text was written by the County Governor of Stockholm, former leader of the conservative party Moderaterna Ulf Adelsohn.

Gamla gubbar ska man ej förakta,

de gör det bra, men de gör det sakta.

Gamla gumman blir på gott humör

för hon är nöjd med vad gubben gör.

You shouldn't despise old men,

they do it well, but they do it slow.

The old lady is in high spirits

for she likes what the old man does.

Jag drömmer

(Mel: Jag väntar vid min stockeld)
This dream comes from the Swedish singer – vissångerska – Margareta Kjellberg.

Jag drömmer om den dagen,

då jag slipper att sjunga

och kan ta mig en sup utan nubbvisa till

och slipper att vara så käck som de unga,

— utan vara så gammal och trist som jag vill!

I'm dreaming of the day

when I don't have to sing

and can have a snaps sans-snaps song

and not have to be as perky as the young,

but be as old and dull as I wish!

Mera brännvin i glasen

(Mel: Internationalen)

Hans Dalborg, former chairman of the board of one of Sweden's largest banks, Nordea, wrote this as a student in 1963. The event was a competition in writing a snaps song in ten minutes. Dalborg won the first prize.

Mera brännvin i glasen,
mera glas på vårt bord,
mera bord på kalasen,
mer kalas på vår jord,
mera jordar med måne,
mera månar i mars,
mera marscher till Skåne,
mera Skåne – bevars!

More snaps in our glasses,
more glasses on our table,
more tables at the party,
more parties on earth,
more planets with a moon,
more moons in March,
more marches to Skåne,
more Skåne[x] — to be sure!

Minne

(Mel: Memory)

One of Finland's great snaps songwriters is Bosse Österberg, an architect in Helsinki. He wrote this text in about 1985. It is now widely spread.

Minne! Jag har tappet mitt minne!
Är jag svensk eller finne?
Kommer inte ihåg.
Inne! Är jag ut' eller inne?
Jag har luckor i minne,
såna där alko-hål.
Men besinne,
man tätar med det brännvin man får,
fastän minnet och helan går!

---

[x]... The brand of akvavit.

Memory! I have lost my memory!
Am I a Swede or a Finn?
I can't remember.
Inside! Am I out' or inside?
I have gaps in my memory,
those small alco-holes.
But know this,
the snaps you get seals your fate,
though memory and The First go.

Om cykling

(Mel: Väva vadmal)

It is said that this is Povel Ramel's only snaps song. At least it is his most well-known. He wrote it in 1964.

Man cyklar för lite,
man röker för mycke,
och man är fasen så liberal
när det gäller maten och spriten!
Jag borde slutat för länge sedan
men denna sup är så liten.
Vad tjänar att hyckla?
Tids nog får man cykla.

You cycle too little,
you smoke too much,
and you're so damned liberal
when it comes to the food and the booze!
I should've quit long ago,
but this snaps is so small.
Why be hypocritical?
Soon enough you'll cycle.

Tiden går

(Mel: Helan går)

Bosse Parnevik, who wrote this is a Swedish comedian and master impersonator. He is the father of U.S. based professional golf player Jesper Parnevik.

//: Tiden går, sjung hoppfallerallanlallanlej. ://
(Töm nu ditt glas fort som f-n)
Och dom som inte hänger me'
får finna sej att ett, tu, tre —
tiden gick! Så ingen snaps dom fick!

//: Time passes, sing hoppfallerallanlallanley. ://
(Now, empty your glass quickly)
And those who are not keeping up
have to face that, one, two three —
The time passed! So, snaps they don't get!

Tänk så mycket gott

(Mel: Kors på Idas grav)

The author is singer-song writer Lasse Dahlquist from Göteborg, best known for his many songs related to Göteborg and to the sea. He wrote it in 1968.

Tänk så mycket gott det kommer ur ett hav
Utan det så skulle silla gå i kvav.
Ja, vad vore lilla nubben ifall silla vore dö.
Öppna käften för nu kommer det en sjö!

Think how much good comes from the sea.
Without it, the herring would founder.
Yes, what little snaps would mean if the herring were dead.
Open your jaws, because here comes a wave!

Än en gång däran

(Mel: Evert Taube's original)

Evert Taube wrote this drinking song in the 1920s. It became the signature song for the "Visans Vänner" association in Stockholm that started in 1936. Evert Taube was one of the founders.

Än en gång däran, bröder,
än en gång däran!
Följom den urgamla seden.
Intill sista man, bröder,
intill sista man
trotsa vi hatet och vreden.

Blankare vapen sågs aldrig i en här
än dessa glasen. Kamrater, i gevär!
Än en gång däran, bröder,
än en gång däran!
Svenska hjärtans djup, här är din sup!

Livet är så kort, bröder,livet är så kort!
Lek det ej bort, nej var redo.
Kämpa mot allt torrt, bröder,
kämpa mot allt torrt!
Tänk på de gamle som skredo
fram utan tvekan i floder av champagne,
styrkta från början av brännvin från vårt land!
Livet är så kort, bröder,
livet är så kort!
Svenska hjärtans djup, här är din sup!

Once again it's time, brothers,
once again it's time!
Let's stick to the ancient custom.
Until the last man, brothers,
until the last man
we defy hatred and anger.
Shinier weapons have never been seen
than these glasses. Comrades, to arms!
Once again it's time, brothers,
once again it's time!
From the bottom of Swedish hearts, here is your drink!

Life is so short, brothers,
life is so short!
Don't dally it away, no, be ready.
Fight all that is dry, brothers,
fight all that is dry!
Think of the old men who glided
forward, without hesitation, in rivers of champagne,
already refreshed by snaps from our country!
Life is so short, brothers,
life is so short!
From the bottom of Swedish hearts, here is your drink!

Snapsvisor for Those Not Drinking

There is no need to drink alcohol at a dinner party where snaps songs are executed, if you don't want to. The most important is to sing and have a good time. If you are a dedicated driver or if you do not like drinking snaps, there are songs for you too.

Vi alla som har kört er hit

(Mel: Vi gå över daggstänkta berg)
Please do not drive if you have a snaps!

Vi alla som har kört oss hit, fallera,
vi avstår helt ifrån att dricka sprit, fallera.
Men om man nu vill truga
får taxi kanske duga,
då lämnar vi bilen med flit, fallera!

All who've driven us here, fallera,
we refrain from drinking alcohol, fallera.
But if you want to push it
a taxi would do it,
then we can leave the car on purpose, fallera!

Mjölkvisa

(Mel: Trink, trink, Brüderlein trink)
This is a song for milk-lovers.

Mjölk, mjölk, vi vill ha mjölk,
det är en underbar dryck.
Mjölk, mjölk, vi vill ha mjölk,
det är vår senaste nyck.
Hämta nu spannen och mjölka din get,
ge mej en klunk utav det.
Slut upp i kampen för helnykterhet,
mjölk är det bästa vi vet!

Milk, milk, we want milk,
it is a wonderful drink.
Milk, milk, we want milk,
that's our latest fancy.
Now, get the bucket and milk your goat,

give me a sip out of it.
Support the fight for teetotalism,
milk is the best we know!

Kaffevisa
(Mel: När månen vandrar)
...and, a song for coffee-lovers written by Swedish author Mauritz Cramaer (1818-1848).

Av allt det goda som man förtär
bland alla jordiska drycker,
ju kaffetåren den bästa är,
den skingrar människans nycker.
Den styrker kroppen, den livar själen,
den känns från hjässan, ja ner i hälen.
//: Halleluja! ://

När hösten kommer med blåst och snö,
när våren börjar sin väta,
då blir till lynnet man kärv och slö,
man vill blott sova och träta.
Ja, man är ruskig i hela kroppen,
men då finns hälsan i kaffekoppen.
//: Halleluja! ://

När färska nyheter månde tas
från stadens hundrade kanter,
man på ett litet honnett kalas
ser sina vänner och tanter.
Vid kaffebordet man gör sitt bästa
med fantiserande om sin nästa.
/:: Halleluja! ://

Of all good things that you consume
among all earthly drinks,
a coffee's drop is the best,
it dispels mankind's fancies.
It strengthens the body, it enlivens the soul,
it is felt from your head down to your sole.
//: Hallelujah! ://

When autumn comes with wind and snow,
when spring begins with rain,
your mood becomes harsh and slow,
you only want for sleep and bickerin'.
Yes, your whole body feels terrible,
but health can be found in a coffee cup.
//: Hallelujah! ://

When fresh news is what you seek
from all corners of town,
then you, at a small, honest party
will see friends and ladies.
At the coffee table they'll do their best
fantasizing about their neighbors.
//: Hallelujah! ://

Kaffe, kaffe

(Mel: Isabella)
One more coffee-song, found on the Internet.

Kaffe, kaffe,
nyss var jag mätt och tung.
Kaffe, kaffe,
gör mej så pigg och ung.
När kaffet i blodet rinner
all åldersgräns försvinner.
Vi ger oss opp
i vals, galopp,
när musiken snart spelar opp!

Coffee, coffee,
recently, I was satisfied and heavy.
Coffee, coffee,
makes me alert and young.
When the coffee flows in the blood
all age limits are gone.
We get up
in waltz, galop,
when the music strikes up!

Vad dom kan göra

(Mel: Mors lilla Olle)

Lättmjölk, folkmjölk and starkmjölk hint at the three types of Swedish beer — each with different alcohol content. "Lättmjölk" (low-fat milk) is a kind of milk that you buy at the grocery store, but "folkmjölk" (folk-milk) and "starkmjölk" (strong-milk) are still to be invented by the dairies.

Vad dom kan göra i vårt mejeri,
mjölk kan dom tillverka med grejer i.
Lättmjölk och folkmjölk och starkmjölk är bra,
dom ska vi dricka i morron, hurra!

Look what they can do in our dairy,
they can make milk of many kinds.
Low-fat milk and folkmjölk and starkmjölk are good,
let's have it all tomorrow morning, hurrah!

Litet glas likt en vas

Mel: Vinden drar

This is for you who are extremely thirsty!

Litet glas
likt en vas
fyllt med blommevann.
Magen är vår slaskespann,
ner med blommevann!

A small glass,
like a vase,
is filled with flower-water.
The stomach is our slop bucket,
pour down the flower-water!

Jag drömmer om en vit vecka

(Mel: White Christmas)

This song is for those who would like to quit drinking.

Jag drömmer om en vit vecka,
sju dagar utan alkohol.
Tänk att bara skåla
i juice och Cola
och sedan minnas allt man gjort!

Jag drömmer om en vit vecka,
det finns en gräns för vad jag tål.
Jag vill inte dricka mer sprit!
Så låt nästa vecka bliva vit.

I'm dreaming of a white week,
seven days without alcohol.
Imagine just toasting
with juice and Cola
and being able to remember all you've done!

I'm dreaming of a white week,
there's a limit of what I can hold.
I don't want to have another drink!
So, let next week become a white one.

Tårtan

(Mel: He'll Be Coming Round the Mountains)
Who said that you have to always sing about alcohol? Maybe you are dreaming about the dessert. The identity of "Frasse" in the song is unclear. You may want to change to the name of the pastry-chef.

Socker, grädde, nötter och så mandelflarn,
inte minst en liten ros av marsipan.
Smörkräm, krikon, snabbkräm och gelé,
en flaska saft och Frasses deg,
och ovanpå lägg på en klick med sylt!

Sugar, cream, nuts and almond cookies,
not the least, a small rose of marzipan.
Buttercream, bullace, fruit cream and jelly,
en flaska safta bottle of juice and Frasse's dough,
and on top, a dollop of jam!

Synonyms of Snaps

In Sweden there is a saying "Kärt barn har många namn", which means roughly "We have many names for the things we love." Well, Swedes love snaps!Some of the synonyms are quite impossible to translate. But they are all words for "snaps", or type of snaps.

Here we go:

Snaps » a small glass containing an alcoholic beverage, often vodka, spiced vodka or aquavit.

A common measure was one "Jungfru" (virgin), about 8.2 cl (2.7 fl oz). It was abandoned in the 1850s. In the mid 1900s a standard size of snaps at restaurants was 7.5 cl (2.5 fl oz). Two of them, a total of 15 cl (5 fl oz) was the allowed ration according to the Swedish alcohol laws at the time. That is, for a man. For a woman the ration was only half as much. Sometimes people ordered "Two white and a brown", meaning two 5 cl glasses of snaps and one of cheap brandy; a total of 15 cl. Later the law was changed so that the standard size of the snaps at restaurants became 6 cl (2 fl oz). In Denmark you may be served a snaps called "en lille en" (a little one). It is quite small, sometimes just 1 cl (0.3 fl oz), which is just a minimal taste.

Blecka (Bläcka) » "Ta sig en bläcka" » "Take a snaps", with an undertone of "Get drunk!"

This expression is old. The original, literal expression was a reference "to have a tin", which referred to the tin measure with which the snaps was measured out, the size of a "Jungfru". It was a hearty snaps, about twice as large as the ordinary vodka shot of today. The spelling "blecka" is sometimes incorrectly changed to "bläcka", or "ett bläck". But it has nothing to do with the word "bläck", which means ink. A snaps of a size of a "blecka" has also been called "kronsup", meaning crown-drink.

Borst » Bristle

Brännvin (Burnt wine) » Snaps

Destillat » Distillate

Dram » Drink
Used by sailors

Drink » Drink

Dunder » Rumble, crash

Fjutt » Kick
A very small one.

Färdknäpp » One for the road

Geting » Wasp

Glas » Glass

Gök » Cuckoo

Halvpanna » Half a kettle, half a bottle

Hemkört » Moonshine

Hutt » Snifter, nip

Jamare » "To have a 'jamare'" means to have a glass of
Jamaica rum.
But the noun "jamare" could also be derived from the verb
"jama" = meow.

Järn » Iron
The material for tin-plate is iron which gave rise to the expres-
sion "ta sig ett järn" (to have an iron). Today it could mean the
drinking of any kind of alcohol.

Jävel » (Devil) Bugger

Klunk » Sip

Klämtare » One who is tolling the bell
But used in this context refers to the glass of snaps.

Knaber » Snaps
The word "knaber" was used in western Sweden to stand for
pebbles to fill pits in roadways. "Knaber", meaning snaps may
have derived from there: Knaber (=snaps) to fill oneself with
(=to get intoxicated).

Knapp » Button

Kröken » (The curve or crook) Booze
It refers to the crooking of your arm when you lift the glass and
move it to your mouth. Therefore "kröken" has become a slang
word for drinking.

Luring » (cheater) Cheat

Morronhutt » Morning nip

Nattkröken » Evening snaps
Most likely a snaps that you have in connection with "nattamat"
or "vickning", a meal served at parties after midnight, or when
you get hungry again several hours after the dinner. We also
have the word "morgonkröken", that could be used if the party
is still going on in the morning hours and you want to start over
again.

Nubbe » From "nubb" = tack
Is a shot of snaps, one of the most common words for a small
alcoholic drink. Because "nubb" is the word for a small nail, the
snaps became "nubbe" because it scratches your throat. The
word was found in printing for the first time in 1892. It was also
used dialectally about farewell snapses and snapses for the
road.

Orre » Cuff

Pilleknarkare » Pill addict.
A smaller snaps.

Pjoltern » Drink

Pärla » Pearl

Rackare » Rogue

Rackabajsare » A substantial snaps
The word is from the German "Rachenbeisser", = halsbitare (throat biter).

Rövare » Robber

Slatt » Heeltap

Skvätt » A few drops

Sprit » Alcohol

Styrkare » Something to fortify yourself

Sup » Snaps, dram, snifter, nip
The most common word for snaps, and the oldest word for "snaps".

Sängfösare » A snaps before you go to bed

Tagel » Horsehair

Taggtråd » Barbed wire.

Tuting » Dram, snifter, nip

Tår » (Tear) Drop

Tår på tand » A drop on the tooth
(Have) a drop, nip. The word "tår" (tear) has in the Swedish language since long ago also had the meaning "a drop of liquid", for instance after coffee – a "kaffe tår", but also about snaps. "Tår på tand" has its origin in the Danish expression "En taar over tørsten" (A drop for the thirst).

Spicing the Snaps

As early as in the 16th century people started to spice their snaps. Not only because it would taste better, but also because some herbs were considered to cure different diseases. Today you don't care much about possible medical advantages — you spice your snaps because it tastes good and makes it more interesting. Some of the more common spices:

Anise (anis)
Beach wormwood (strandmalört), *Artemisia maritima*
Besk — see Wormwood
Blackberries (björnbär)
Black currant berries (svarta vinbär) — was at one point considered good for pain (guaranteed so when used as spice for snaps). Try "svarta vinbärs" with game or with sweet desserts!
Blueberries (blåbär)
Bog myrtle (pors), *Myrica gale*. People believed that this herb was dangerous. It was used to make magic potions. Today we know better. "Porsbrännvin" is delicious with shellfish and herring.
Chamomile (kamomill), *Matricaria recutita*
Caraway (kummin) — was considered good for the stomach. Test caraway spiced snaps with spicy food!
Chervil (körvel) — was considered good for the throat and the stomach.
Cherries (körsbär)
Coriander (koriander). This is an excellent spice together with caraway and fennel. You'll get a snaps that fits with almost anything on the Swedish smörgåsbord.
Dill (dill) — good with seafood, a classic for the crayfish party.
Elderberries (fläder), Sambucus nigra. Perfect with salmon and shellfish.
Enbär — cured aches and coughs.
Fennel (fänkål)
Ginger (ingefära) — good with sushi.
Heather (ljung)
Hops (humle), *Humulus lupulus*. People at one point believed that if you spiced the snaps with hops, the state of intoxication would increase.
Juniper berry (enbär)

Lemon Balm or Balm mint (Citronmeliss), *Melissa officinalis*. Try this snaps with shellfish, Asian food and even with desserts.

Licorice (lakrits). Dissolve your favorite licorice in vodka.

Pepper (peppar) — was used for colic.

Pine shoots (tallskott)

Rowanberries (rönnbär)

Sage (salvia), *Salvia divinorum*. Gave appetite, fastened up loose teeth and cured coughs.

Seville orange peel (pomerans). Works well with meatballs and other meat dishes. Excellent also with dark chocolate.

Sloe berries (slånbär)

Southernwood (åbrodd), *Artemisia abrotanum*.

St. Johns Wort (johannesört), *Hypericum maculatum*. Use only this, the so-called square-shaped St. Johns Wort. It was considered good for all pains. It even protected against "the devil's onsets." In the center of Copenhagen (the "Strøget") at the end of the 1940s, people could buy St. Johns Wort-spiced snaps in bottles with "Against Devilry and Destruction" printed in red letters. Today we enjoy this snaps with most food, specially grilled chicken and the Swedish specialty "pyttipanna" (hash of fried diced meat with onions and potatoes).

Thyme (timjan)

Wild strawberries (smultron)

Wormwood (malört), *Artemisia absinthium* — was considered an excellent stomach medicin. It still is! It also was considered salutary if you have a hangover. This snaps is generally called "Bäsk" (bitter). It is delicious with most foods – if you like it!

Yarrow (rölleka), *Achillea millefolium* — was commonly used for pain and other affections.

Spicing suggestions

If you use a herb such as wormwood, beach wormwood, southernwood, lemon balm, bog myrtle, yarrow or thyme, you should preferably use a flowering sprig. You can also use air-dried sprigs. Put the sprig into an empty half-liter bottle and fill it with un-spiced, 80 proof vodka. The secret to get adequately spiced vodka is to test frequently. It can be ready after a day or two, but sometimes it will take weeks, especially if you make the snaps on berries. You can also keep it for weeks or months to get a concentrate.

Besk (Bäsk)

Swedish Systembolaget's "Beska droppar" is one of its bestsellers in the province of Skåne. But Besk is a bit controversial. Some people say that it is the worst snaps they ever had, undrinkable. Others say that it is the best snaps of them all. (I agree). You do not need to use complicated recipes to get a good Besk. Simply take a sprig of the bush Artemisia absinthium, with or without flowers, put it in an empty half-bottle, fill with unseasoned vodka (or "renat" which is the term for the un-spiced aquavit prior to vodka) and keep it for a few days. The secret is to test it every day until you get the taste and strength you want. You can also keep it until it gets extremely strong (a concentrate) to use whenever you want, at which point you mix it with unseasoned vodka to the taste you prefer. If you want to make a mild, greenish spring-besk you have to harvest the first leaves of the wormwood bush.

That will give a different, milder — to may people more pleasant — taste to the besk.

Black Currant Snaps

To get a great black currant snaps you need to fill a bottle half full with ripe black currant berries. Then add a teaspoon of sugar and fill with vodka. Keep it in the bottle for a month. Then strain. The snaps will have an appealing ruby-red color.

Hjärtansfröjd, Lemon balm snaps

This is a snaps spiced with the young leaves from the lemon balm. You'll get a drink that a long time ago was said "to drive away melancholia, prevent gray hair, cure bee-stings and be overall salutary for the appetite and the digestion." Put a hand-full of flowering sprigs and 50 cl unseasoned vodka in a bottle. Keep for ten days in a dark and cool place. Then strain and put a couple of fresh leaves in the bottle as decoration.

Hypericum

This snaps, which is spiced with the square St. John's Wort, is called "Hypericum", or sometimes jokingly "Hirkumpirkum". You have to fill at least one third of half-a-bottle with the petals from this plant. Then fill it up with vodka and keep it for two weeks. Some recipes call for adding a piece of ginger in the bottle. The snaps will have a wonderful ruby-red color.

Rowanberry snaps

Fill an empty half-bottle with rowanberries. They do not have to be frost-nipped, which many recipes call for. Pour as much vodka as there is room for and keep it for three weeks. Then strain and taste. This snaps is wonderful, especially with wild fowl. Its taste is characterized as sour, fresh, flowery, round, wild and – in my opinion - quite delightful.

Remember, experimenting and frequent tasting is key to appropriately spicing your snaps.

Websites

www.rygert.se
www.spritmuseum.se
www.vinsprit.se
www.snapsvisor.nu
www.snapsvisor.eu
www.spritakademien.se
www.wikipedia.org (or .se for Swedish specific results)
Google: "snapsvisans historia," "sjunga snapsvisa," "snapsvisor" and "nubbevisor"

Sources, literature

••• Attorp, Kaj: Lilla snapsviseboken. Bokförlaget Lind & Co., 2003.

••• Dahlman, Hans: Kändisarnas snapsvisor. Bokförlaget Känguru, 2010.

••• Fischer & Co/Vin & Sprithistoriska Museet: Stora snapsviseboken. Stockholm, 1994.

••• Fischer & Co.: Vi vill ha mera öl. 1996.

••• Fäger, Jan & Rygert, Göran: Sångboken. Chalmerska Ingenjörsföreningen, Göteborg, 2007.

••• Föreningen Gamla Västar: Chalmers Spexikon, Göteborg 1998.

••• Gylder, Ragnvi: Skål alla vänner. B. Wahlströms Bokförlag, 1972.

••• Lindskog, Claes:Malört och vin.

- Läsförlaget AB: Svenska snapsvisor. 1990.

- Mannerström, Leif: Mannerströms sill & strömming. Norstedts, 2012.

- Mattsson, Christina: Från Helan till lilla Manasse. Den svenska snapsvisans histora. Bokförlaget Atlantis, Stockholm, 2002.

- Mattsson, Christina: Helan går.Bokförlaget Atlantis, Stockholm, 2002.

- Meldal, Elsa: Article about spicing snaps.

- Rygert, Göran: Bellmans Bästa. Warner/Chappell Music Scandinavia AB, 1999.

- Rygert, Göran: Festvisor. Warner/Chappell Music Scandinavia AB, Stockholm, 1994.

- Rygert, Göran: Visor för törstiga. Intersong, Stockholm, 1980.

- Rygert, Göran: Visor kring bordet. Warner/Chappell Music Scandinavia AB, Stockholm, 1993.

- Rygert, Göran: The Very Best of Swedish Schnapps Songs. Nordstjernan Förlag, New York, 2008.

- Sandklef, Albert: 30 sorters kryddat brännvin. Bokförlaget Fabel, 1965.

- Små Visor till Stora Supar. Brummel & Co., Helsinki, 1947.

- Spritakademien, Stockholm.

- Spritmuseum, Stockholm. (Formerly Vin- & Sprithistoriska Museet)

- Svenskt visarkiv, Stockholm.

- Swahn, Jan-Öjvind: Vem sade skål här vid bordet (Preface of "Visor kring bordet").

- Toinette, Ann: Article about spicing snaps.

- Widerberg, Bertil: Article about spicing snaps.

- Williams Förlag: Glada nubbevisor. Bromma 1973.

- Wikipedia.

- Åberg, Lasse & Söderqvist, Åke: Nu tar vi den. Askild & Kärnekulls Förlag AB, Stockholm, 1977.

Alphabetical List of Songs

A Mouthful of Vodka 73

Apps & schnapps 49

A Word From the Snaps 73

Bordeaux, Bordeaux 79

Brännvinslåten (Få, få) 24

Bumble-Bees 73

Byssan lull 59

Börsras 47

Den lilla halvan 44

Den är dess skydd i gula faror (August Strindberg) 9

Det var en lördags aften 80

Do It My Way 73

Du ska få mitt gamla snapsglas 60

E lancor 30

En droppe vatten 60

Festen är slut 46

Five Ounces 74

Fordom odlade man vindruvsranka 60

För att mänskan ska 61

Första supen är redan nerklämd 61

Gamla gubbar 80

Getting Tipsy In a Bar 74

Get Your Glasses 50

Gjut brännvin i din strupa 58

Gustafs skål (C.M. Bellman) 23, 25

Hal and Gore 30

Har du något i flaskan kvar (C.M. Bellman) 26

Hej! fram med öl och tallestrunt (C.M. Bellman) 25

Hej, tomtegubbar 62

Helan går 28, 29

Helan kommer, helan går 63

Icke nu! 45

I Finlands djupa skogar 63

I Like the Snaps 74

Imbelupet glaset står 64

In My Belly 74

I See a Small One 75

It's a Long Way 75

Jag drömmer om den dagen 80

Jag drömmer om en vit vecka 88

Jag hade en snaps en gång 64

Kaffe, kaffe 87

Kaffevisa 86

Korta solen 52

Kräftans tröst 47

Krök armen i vinkel 65

Life Is a Pleasure 75

Litet glas, likt en vas 88

Little, Little Vodka 75

Livet är härligt 41, 65

Långt ner i Småland 65

Mera brännvin i glasen 81

Min lilla lön 66

Minne 81

Mjölkvisa 85

Måsen 66

Now For the First 30

Nubben är en form av spriten 55

Number One a Pleasure Was 76

Nuuuuu!!! 45

När helan man tagit 67

Oh, When the Schnapps 76

Old Mac Donald 76

Om cykling 82

Papa Loves Vodka 49

Punschen kommer 67

Schnapps and Beer 76

Ser du stjärnan i det blå 44

Slå i, slå i 44

Snille och snaps 48

There's a Place In a Bar 77

The Swedish Cook 77

Tiden går 83

Till supen så tager man sill 68

To Improve Your Appetite 77
Tomma glas i gott kalas 68
Tomodachi 31
Tur och retur 48
Twinkle, Twinkle, Vodka Bar 78
Tårtan 89
Tänk om jag hade lilla nubben 69
Tänk så mycket gott 83
Törsten rasar 69
Utan smärta 70
Uti min mage 70
Vad dom kan göra 88
Van Gogh 45
Vi alla som kört er hit 85
Vodka, Vodka 78
Vodka zdyes 31
What a Vodka 77
When I Get Drunker 78
You Can Have Another Yet 78
You'll Inherit My Shotglass 78
Å sella ho går i havet 71
Än en gång däran 83
Än går det vågor i halvankaren 71